Giving Away My Millions

Published in the United Kingdom by NJF Books
First Published in 2019

Copyright © Tom Jones / Nick Fisher
All rights reserved

ISBN 978-0-9932361-6-7

Acknowledgements

I would like to thank Nick Fisher for his help (and extreme patience) in writing this book. If it wasn't for our chance meeting this book would never have been written. I'd also like to thank my wife for standing by me through the good times and through the *very* good times! Fortunately, there have been no bad. I dedicate this book to her and our four wonderful children. I also dedicate this book to my dad, who without his help, guidance and advice I wouldn't be in the very privileged position I am today.

Contents

Foreword

If you were stood at a ticket machine on a car park and someone who was driving a £150,000 car asked you for a pound for a ticket because they didn't have any change would you give it to them? And if you gave it to them and they gave you £100 in return what would you think? Or if you were filling up your car at a petrol station and when you went in to pay you were told that someone had already paid for your petrol for you and then the cashier handed you a twenty pound note, how would you react? And if you were walking down the street and a complete stranger walked up to you and gave you an envelope and said, "I think this is yours," and walked off. And when you opened it you found a thousand pounds inside, what would you do?

Well if any of those things *did* happen to you you'd probably be taken slightly by surprise and no doubt you wouldn't know quite what to say or do, but either way it'd certainly brighten your day up. And that's what I like to do, brighten people's day up, and I do this by giving money to complete strangers. Sometimes I'll give them £100 or £200, other times I'll give them £500 or a £1,000. I've given much larger amounts away too, including half a million in one go. I've also paid off debts of several thousand pounds for people, paid for a family to go to Disney World in Florida, paid for another family's holiday in Spain, put a homeless person up in a hotel, bought an elderly couple a £600 flat screen television in Curry's (and paid for a three years extended warranty on it for them that cost *another* three hundred quid that like all the other extended warranties that sales assistants try and talk you into buying they'll probably never claim on!) I've withdrawn money from cash dispensers outside banks and deliberately left it in the machine for people to find, gone into shops and hidden money inside clothes and books for other people to find, came to the rescue of a woman and her son at the airport and paid for their flights to Canada (business class) after the flight they were on was overbooked, sent money totalling £40,000 inside Christmas cards to people I'd never seen, gave a woman I saw in Tesco's who was full of a cold the money to take the day off work, and I once bought someone an ice cream in the Lake District. "Oh how very generous of him," you all sarcastically say, "He bought someone an ice cream!" Well at nearly three quid each and considering that not only did I buy the person behind me a Mr Wippy but the other thirty or so people in the queue too, it *was* fairly generous of me actually as it cost me the best part of seventy quid! And these people and the countless others who I've given money to all had one thing in common - they'd never clapped eyes on me before in their entire life. And bar one, well two actually, they haven't since.

Chapter One A Hundred And Fifty Million Reasons To Give My Money Away

First of all I have a confession to make; my name isn't Tom Jones. I've used a pseudonym. And one of the reasons I decided to use a pseudonym to write this book instead of writing it using my real name was because as it's about me giving money away I didn't want people to think I'd done it for attention or for some kind of publicity. Far from it, I'd much rather remain anonymous, hence using the name 'Tom Jones'. And I also thought that if I used my real name some people might think I'm being flash and big-headed, like, 'Hey, look at me. My name is **** ******* and I'm fabulously rich and what a great guy I am giving all this money away to people' kind of thing, which isn't the case at all. It's just that I'd much prefer to share my story with people, which hopefully they'll find interesting, without anyone knowing who I am. Although there are a few, around a dozen or so close friends plus members of my family who *do* know my identity.

Another reason for not using my real name is because as I'm still in the process of giving my money away, if everyone knew who I really was I'd end up with a queue of people ten miles long outside my house! I've also kept my identity secret for my own safety because as I sometimes have large amounts of cash on me I'd be putting myself at risk of being attacked or mugged. Hardly a day goes by these days when you don't read in the newspaper that someone has been robbed on the street and have had their wallet, handbag or mobile phone taken from them. Or a pensioner has been beaten up in their own home for little more than a few pounds. And if some unscrupulous person, of which unfortunately there are many in our society, were to know there was someone like myself walking around with several thousand pounds in cash on them I'd be a very easy target for them and no doubt sooner or later I too would end up appearing in the column of a newspaper being reported on as a victim of street crime. And so after taking all this into account I thought it best to write using a pseudonym under the name Tom Jones.

I was originally going to use the name *Jack* Jones which I thought may be rather appropriate considering that when I'm out and about giving money to people I usually am 'on my Jack Jones' as the saying goes. But as I was driving to Cardiff one day I went through a town in Wales called

Pontypridd where the singer Tom Jones hails from, who in my opinion is one of the greatest singers of all time and who is one of my favourites, and I just so happened to be playing one of his CD's in my car at the time. And as I was thinking about him a pun came into my head that I thought I might be able to use somewhere in this book. So instead of writing it under the name *Jack* Jones I decided to write it under the name *Tom* Jones, though I thought it best to drop the 'Sir' part! Mind you, rather like *my* real name isn't Tom Jones, 'Tom Jones' isn't Tom Jones's real name either. But I think both this book and Tom's songs have more of a ring to them than they would if they were titled 'by Thomas John Woodward' (Tom's real name) don't you think?

But even though my *name* may be false the accounts and stories of how I give money away to complete strangers aren't. You may well find some of the stories hard to believe, bizarre even, but I assure you that every one of the stories is true, though my wife still can't quite believe the one where I once paid for a woman and her young son to fly business class to Canada when I'd only just met her ten minutes previously at the airport! Which I'll tell you about a little later on.

So what made me want to start giving money away to complete strangers?

Well first of all I think I've got too much money. Some people, mainly elitist's and the wealthiest of the wealthy will say that you can *never* have too much money but to me I think that's a ludicrous thing to say because there's only so much money you can spend in a lifetime. I'm a millionaire many, many times over, and including property I own and other business interests and assets I have, I'm worth in excess of £150 million. That's a ridiculous amount of money for *anyone* to have. It's *too* much money in fact, far too much for just one person (and their family) to have. And even though I've worked hard for it and invested wisely to accumulate it and I enjoy the benefits of having such a huge amount, I still think it's far too much. Me, my wife and our four kids could live our lives ten times over in the manner we do and we'd still never get around to spending it all. So despite some people saying you can never have enough money there does become a point when you can end up with too much. Or at least with more than you'll need or more than you're ever going to spend anyway. And on top of the property, business interests, investments and other assets I have, plus all the money I have in the bank, I also own several luxury cars including a Lamborghini and a Ferrari which are worth a couple of million between them. Though more often than not I drive a Bentley Continental which cost 'slightly' less at just over £150,000, and my wife drives a Range Rover SVAutobiography which cost a similar price. We live in a house that is worth in the region of £8.5 million that has its own cinema and indoor swimming pool and I've got paintings hanging on the walls that are worth hundreds of thousands of pounds. We regularly go on luxury holidays. We stay in five star hotels wherever we go and we travel first class *when*ever we go (sometimes we even charter a private jet depending on the destination.) And I own my own yacht and my kids go to a private school. We really do live a fantastic lifestyle and I couldn't ask for more out of life.

I'm not boasting about the lifestyle I have or being the flash big head some people may think I'm being. I'm just trying to give you an insight into the kind of life I lead and how wealthy I am and how I came into it.

To a degree you could say I was 'born' into it although I didn't actually become a millionaire until I was thirty five years old. And to be honest I'm not quite a *self made* millionaire either. That's because when I first started out I got a helping hand from my dad who was fairly well off himself. So from a young age I've been used to a somewhat lavish lifestyle.

My dad made his money from a chain of shoe repairers, or 'cobblers' as they were more commonly known as in those days, that he built up and later sold. So as well as being fairly wealthy you could also say my dad was well heeled! As were all our shoes when we were kids. The only downside was that we never got a new pair - he just kept on repairing the old ones! And with now having four kids myself and with the price of kids shoes - particularly school shoes - being the best part of £70 nowadays, I sometimes wish I'd followed in my dad's footsteps and become a cobbler myself.

However, even though I was assisted by my dad in making my first million I've since made many millions more entirely by myself. Although in the first instance of making my own million it was more down to good fortune than having good business sense.

I started off investing in the housing market in the mid 1980's and I bought one or two properties in London. The timing of me buying them was perfect because unbeknown to anyone at the time the property boom was just around the corner and when it arrived and property prices started to rocket I literally made millions overnight. Well, perhaps not overnight, it was more like over the next couple of years. Nevertheless, it was still a very short space of time to make such a huge return on my investments.

But it was just pure luck really. Like I say, I just happened to buy property at the right time and nobody knew or could have predicted that house prices were going to increase by as much and as quickly as they did. And it didn't slow down. Property prices just continued to rise - and then rise even more. And then even when house prices *did* eventually start to level out and the housing market began to settle down, in some places, particularly in London, prices continued to increase.

The housing boom of the mid to late eighties took everyone by surprise. Not even the most optimistic of estate agents (and most estate agents are VERY optimistic, none more so than those that sell investment property. I think some are *fantasists* not optimists with the prices they come up with) could have imagined that the value of property would rise so sharply like it did back then. It was possibly the best time ever to buy property anywhere in the UK although if someone had said to you at the time that the house you were buying would double or triple in value within a few years you'd have said they were having a laugh. But if you *did* buy a house at that time, a few years later *you'd* be the one laughing - all the way to the bank. And if you bought a house in London, or two or three houses like *I* did, then not only would've you been *laughing* all the way to the bank you'd have been doing cartwheels all the way there too like I was. And I wouldn't have been the only one cart wheeling down to the NatWest. Many others would have made a million or two out of that particular property boom. In fact, anyone, investors and first or second time buyers alike who bought property in London for around half a million at the same time I did would have also seen the value of their house triple, or quadruple even in some cases, making them a millionaire too in the process. Even if only on paper.

For instance, I purchased one house for £525,000 and within eighteen months it had tripled in value to over £1.5 million. Three years later it was worth £3.5 million. The same house is now valued at over *five* million. That's a tenfold increase. And I still own it. The other two houses that I bought back then for around the same price also increased in value by similar margins. I sold those two around ten years later and made nearly £2,500,000 on each one.

Looking back I wish I'd had bought five or six houses and not just two or three, though I have bought property in the London area since then that I still own and which I rent out. I also own property in New York and Dubai as well as a villa in Southern Spain and I've got a caravan in North Wales! Seriously! I *really do* have a caravan in North Wales, in Anglesey. It's not the type that's got wheels on it and you hook to the back of your car and drive to different campsites with it, which I wouldn't be able to do anyway because my Lamborghini hasn't got a tow bar, it's a *static* caravan. It's more of a lodge actually but it's still sited on a caravan park - surrounded by caravans on wheels!

So it's fair to say that financially my future is secure. More importantly so are my kid's futures, which to me - and probably like what most other parents strive and wish for - is the most important thing of all.

We truly are very fortunate and I always remind my kids of how fortunate they are too and not to take *anything* for granted (like *my* dad always used to remind me.) And to be fair, they don't. They want for nothing but they appreciate it. However not all wealthy people (including some I know personally) and some celebrities you read about treat their kids the same way as I do mine. Some have a totally different attitude when it comes to giving money and sharing their wealth with their children. You read of some celebrities who say they give their kids hardly anything and how their kids shouldn't expect anything from them to help give them a start in life and that they should work for it like they had to. And you also often read stories of how some rich people say that they don't intend to leave their kids anything at all when they die. Not a penny. But who else are they going to leave it to? Who else is there in your life that is more important than your own kids? No-one. So why *wouldn't* anyone want to leave everything to them or help give them a start in life. My dad did it for me and it did me no harm and I'm going to do it for my kids too. And I'm sure that ninety nine point nine percent of parents would do it for their kids as well if they could afford it.

I really can't understand why anyone who is extremely wealthy wouldn't want to help their kids get off to a good start in life or leave anything for them in their will. And as long as your kids respect and appreciate what you do for them I can't see the problem with spending money on them and giving them a luxurious life style or helping them financially when they begin to make their own way in life. My four have already got a bank account each with £250,000 in each one, although they can't access it until they're eighteen. It's more of a trust fund actually than it is a bank account and me and my wife can't access it either, only the kids when they come of age. And I've done this so that in the highly unlikely event that I was to lose everything tomorrow at least my kid's futures are taken care of. But some wealthy parents wouldn't even give their kids two hundred and fifty quid let alone two hundred and fifty thousand. And you read of some wealthy celebrities that won't even pay for their kids to sit next to them in first class on a plane when they travel and they bung them in economy. I wouldn't dream - and probably neither would most parents - of making my kids sit in economy class on a flight whilst I sat in first class like Gordon Ramsey says he does. What a tight arse!

But each to their own as they say and every parent brings their own kids up differently and I'm not saying that my way is the right way, it's just *my* way. Though I must admit there have been times when I've felt like sticking my youngest at the back of the plane as far away as possible from first class when she has one of her tantrums mid flight!

But when you've amassed the kind of wealth that I have you could fly first class every day of the week, stay in five star hotels every night, have luxury holidays once a month and have a different coloured Ferrari for every day of the week and you'd still have millions left in your bank account that you'll never get around to spending. So once you're in that position and you know that you and your family's futures are taken care of financially, what else is there to do with your money? And I was thinking about this one day and I thought, 'I know. I'll give some of it away!' And two years ago that's what I started to do. I didn't have a figure in mind of what the total amount I'd be giving away was going to be, and I still don't. I just decided one day that I'd give some of it away.

But despite me having no idea of what the total amount I was going to give away would be and in what denominations I'd give it, I did have an idea in mind of who I intended to give it away to. And that idea was to give it to complete strangers, though as well as having the intention of giving it to complete strangers I also intended on giving some of it to friends too. But unlike having no idea of the amount and in what denominations to give to those who I didn't know, I had exact figures in mind of the first five amounts I'd give away and whom to give it to.

Chapter Two Well, There's Half A Million Gone, Now How Do I Give Away Some More?

I've always been quite generous towards my friends and family. For example on my 40th birthday I took five of my closest friends to New York for five nights and then from New York we flew to Las Vegas for a further five nights. I paid for everything. Flights, hotels, food, drink, restaurant bills, the lot. I even sent them champagne to their seats in economy class from my seat in first class where I was sat on the flight over there. Only joking! We *all* travelled first class and on every leg of the journey. They didn't have to spend a penny. Not even in the casinos as I gave them all spending money of $500 each night we were there.

The total cost of the trip was around £70,000 and we had an absolutely fantastic time. It was even more fantastic for one of my friends because he won over $4,000 on the last night in the casino at the hotel we were staying in, the Bellagio in Las Vegas. He insisted I took the winnings because I'd given him the money to play with in the first place but I refused to take it. But the fact that he offered it meant a lot to me and just goes to show what a true friend he is.

However, even though I've taken friends, and on occasions *friends* of friends that I hardly knew, on trips abroad and treated them in various other ways, I've never actually given them money. So when I decided to start giving some of it away the five friends who I took to New York and Vegas were the first one's I gave it to. These five were (and still are) the closest of all my friends so I thought who better to give it to.

I'd already decided that I was going to give them some money and I'd already decided on the amount, so one night I invited them around to my house. I told them of my intentions of how I was going to start giving money away and that I was going to give it to complete strangers and that I wanted them to help by coming up with different ideas of how to do it. I then said that as well as giving it to strangers I was also going to give it to people I knew, namely them, and I handed them an envelope each and when they opened it they couldn't quite believe their eyes because inside was a cheque for £100,000 each.

Now at this point the odd few reading this may well be thinking, "I don't believe him. He's making this up. Nobody gives half a million pounds away. Not even to their closest friends." But believe me,

I'm not making *any* of it up although when I gave each of them a cheque for £100,000 they couldn't quite believe it themselves!

But if for some reason you're *not* totally convinced that I'm telling the truth and that I didn't really give half a million away in one go, then this may put things into perspective.

If you won the lottery this Saturday, say £6 million, would you give your best friends some of the money? Of course you would! You might not give them as much as £100,000 each but I'm sure you'd take care of the friends that are closest to you and give them something. And if you *do* win £6 million on the lottery this Saturday and you *don't* give your best friends anything then you're a right tight arse like Gordon Ramsey!

Out of £6 million you could quite easily afford to give £100,000 each to five of your best friends *plus* give another half a million to family members and it'd still leave you with £5 million. And you could live very comfortably for the rest of your life with the five million you've got left I'm sure.

So with me being worth around *one hundred and fifty* million, for me to give away £500,000 in one go to five of *my* best friends is nothing at all really as I too can continue to live very comfortably for the rest of my life with what I have left.

Don't get me wrong, it's a hell of a lot of money - and it's a hell of a lot to give away - but it's a drop in the ocean to someone like me and it won't impact on me financially one bit. Furthermore, I'll probably recoup double or treble that amount on future business investments. And even if I didn't recoup it, it wouldn't make any difference because like I say, I'll never get around to spending all my money anyway so I may as well give such a large amount away. And in comparison to someone giving away £500,000 out of a six million pound lottery win, which no doubt some lottery winners have done, not only is giving away £500,000 a drop in the ocean to me, it's a *tiny* drop in the ocean because it still leaves me with £149.5 million.

Hopefully after me explaining it like that, if there were one or two reading this that didn't believe I gave my friends half a million between them, you do now. And if you still don't believe me then you're certainly not going to believe some of the example's you'll read of how I've given money away. But then again you won't be alone. Because looking back even *I* can't believe I did some of them!

Yet when I handed the cheques to my five

friend's and they saw how much it was for, just like the one that said I should take his winnings from the casino in Las Vegas, each one of them said they couldn't take it and handed it back to me. They said they didn't want my money and that it was my friendship that mattered most and even if I wasn't as wealthy as I am and I had no money at all they'd still be my friends. And I know they meant it. But just like I refused to take my friends winnings from the casino, I also refused to take their cheques back, though it did take some persuading for them to keep it.

Ironically, one of those who I gave a cheque to didn't need the money because like myself he too is a millionaire several times over. But I could hardly give four of them a hundred grand each and give him nothing could I. If I did that he'd be nicknaming *me* 'Gordon'! (I hope Gordon Ramsey isn't reading this otherwise he might lace my food with poison next time I call in his Maze Grill in Mayfair. But then again if he does read it, it might prompt him into flying his kids first class with him next time he jets over from L.A.)

So after persuading my five friends to accept the cheques (and it really did take some persuading) we sat down and discussed different ideas of how to give it to people.

They asked me how much I was planning on giving away and I said that I had no idea and that I really hadn't thought about figures or how much. And I said that barring the half a million that I'd just given to *them* it could be a further half a million or it could be one or two million. I really had no idea.

So we started to bounce ideas about of how to give it away and one suggestion was to give it away in lump sums to needy charities such as giving £10,000 to a charity for the homeless, which wasn't a bad idea as it'd be going to a good cause, like most charities are. But then one of my other friends said that rather than give a lump sum of £10,000 to a homeless charity, perhaps a better idea would be to give £100 each to a hundred different homeless people living on the streets of London (which was the nearest city) which we all thought made more sense as it'd certainly brighten up a homeless person's day if someone walked up to them and gave them a hundred quid. And that was one of the reasons for doing it after all, to brighten up people's day and put a smile on their face. The only slight drawback with doing something like that is that you don't really know if the person who you are giving the money to is genuinely homeless or not as a lot aren't, and it's impossible to distinguish who is and who isn't. The vast majority you see *are* but quite a few are just pretending to be homeless and treat sitting on the streets asking for money as some kind of job and then go home at night. And a lot of local councils are now advising people against giving money to those they see on the streets and if anything to buy them a cup of coffee or a sandwich instead, which is probably a better idea. Although from my point of view it'd be much easier just to give two £50 notes to every homeless person I saw than it would walking around London with a tray of sandwiches and a flask!

That reminds me of a funny story I once read in the newspaper when a woman thought she'd help an old tramp she'd seen by buying him some cigarettes. She'd walked past this bloke and saw him picking up a 'dimp' (the end of a cigarette with not much left on it) off the pavement and so she went into a newsagent's and very kindly bought him a packet of Benson and Hedges and went outside to give them to him. But as she went to hand them to him he looked at them and said, "I don't smoke Benson's," and turned his back on her and walked off and left her stood there holding them! She must have thought, 'You cheeky bastard!' Well even tramps have preferences I suppose.

So we decided that giving money direct to a homeless person was probably a better idea than giving it to a homeless charity. At least that way they could buy the right brand of cigarettes they smoked! It also gave me an idea along the same lines, as you'll see.

After discussing it further we also decided that as well as giving it out at say a hundred pounds at a time to homeless people as opposed to giving a large lump sum of £10,000 to a homeless *charity*, it would also be better to give it away in similar amounts all around. It didn't take much working out that if I gave away £10,000 at a time, if I was to give that to just fifty people it would amount to half a million pounds. But it wasn't the half a million pounds that it amounted to I'd be giving away that was the issue. It was the fact that only fifty people would benefit from it. Whereas by doing it the other way around and giving people £100 each, instead of just *fifty* people benefiting, *five thousand* people would benefit and I'd still be giving away the same amount, half a mil'. As it turned out, on many occasion I gave away *more* than £100 at a time, sometimes a *lot* more. Or as you'll see in the one about the friendly traffic warden, a lot less! Though initially I did start off giving away £100 at a time.

One of my friends said that the only problem with giving it away in smaller amounts might be the length of time it took to give it away. But as I explained to him, just like I didn't have a figure in mind of the amount I intended to give away, I hadn't put a time scale on it either. I said that I might do it for one year or I might do it for ten, or that I might even get fed up doing it after six months, who knows?

So we did a quick calculation, and based on giving just four people £100 a day every day of the week for twelve months, it equated to £146,000 a year I'd be giving away. Obviously I wouldn't be doing it every single day. It'd be like having a full time job giving money away if I did! So what he said was right. It may well take quite a while to give a substantial amount away. And by 'substantial' I mean around the half a million that'd already been mentioned, not that a £146,000 itself isn't a substantial amount to give away, because it certainly is.

I could've quite easily given it away a lot quicker by just standing on a street corner in the town centre handing £100 out to everyone that passed by. But apart from the security aspect that I was a bit concerned about - stood there with large amounts of cash on me - there'd be no real 'fun' in giving it away like that. Because as well as wanting to put a smile on someone's face by giving them a few quid I also wanted to surprise them a little bit too, which as you'll find out I certainly did. And not only was everyone taken by surprise, most were totally shocked. And quite a few nearly fainted!

So we chatted about it a bit more and said that over the next few weeks whenever we had an idea of how to give money to someone that would take them totally by surprise we'd write it down. And we came up with some absolute belters. We also said that taking into account the length of time it would take to give a significant amount away it might also be an idea to give more than £100 away at a time. Although regarding the surprise element I suppose we needn't have bothered writing down different ideas of how to give it someone because in *any* circumstance if someone you'd never met before walked up to you and gave you a hundred, two hundred or a *thousand pounds* even, as I ended up doing in some cases, you'd be surprised no matter *how* it was given to you. You'd be surprised if someone walked up to you and gave you *twenty* quid for no reason, let alone a hundred or a thousand!

So over the following few weeks we made a list of ways of how to go about it and when I eventually began doing it I used quite a few of the ideas we'd come up with. But then after a while, most of the time I did it I just did it on the spur of the moment with no specific way in mind of how I was going to go about it. Some days I might have been out and about doing whatever it was I had to do with no intention whatsoever of giving money away on that particular day and I'd do something that was so spur of the moment it even took me by surprise never mind the person I was giving it to! Yet on other days I *did* go out with a specific way in mind of how I was going to do it, like on the car parks for instance.

When I gave people the money most of their reactions were the same, disbelief, though I didn't always see a person's reaction. And as well as reacting with disbelief some were slightly cautious, as you might be if a complete stranger had just given you a handful of twenty pound notes or a couple of fifties for no reason whatsoever. And most asked the same questions such as, 'Why?' or 'What's that for?' And I'd just say the first thing that came into my head like 'It's for you!' or 'I just felt like giving it to you, that's all.' And several asked, "Is this a wind up?" and I'd just reply "No, it's not a wind," and smile and walk off. And if you're wondering why in some cases I didn't always see a person's reaction after they'd got the money, it's because as well as physically handing money to people, I/we also discretely hid it in places I knew where it would be easily found. I say 'we' and not just 'I' because on occasions I was aided by my five friends, though ninety percent of the time I was by myself. And probably around ninety percent of the time too, a lot of the people who received the money or who found it probably weren't even in need of it. Although at times we did go out of our way to make sure that those who we thought may be in need of it, like the homeless and the not so well off, got it. And quite possibly they appreciated it more than most. But having said that, I'm sure that *everyone* who received something appreciated it a great deal.

This isn't the first time something like this has been done, though it may well be the first time someone has written a book about it, I don't know. And I'm sure you've heard similar stories of wealthy people giving their money away too. It happens all the time and isn't uncommon. Though perhaps doing it the way I do it isn't as common as the way other wealthy people give it away. Some give million pound donations to the Conservative or Labour parties. Others will leave hundreds of thousands of pounds to their local cat's home. Personally, I wouldn't give money to either of them because I haven't got much time for politicians and I can't stand cats. Come to think of it, cats and politicians do have one thing in common. Cats have the annoying habit of coming through your garden gate and wandering up your path towards your front door - as does your local MP at election time - even though you'd much rather both didn't. And once in your garden shit tends to come out of both of them. One will just stand on your path and blatantly shit on it and the other will stand on your path and just blatantly *talk* shit on it. The difference is, a cat will scurry off back down the path again and piss off when you take the appropriate steps to get rid of it, whereas a politician isn't so easy to get shut of. Perhaps in future I should try hurling a bucket of cold water over my local MP followed by a swift kick up the arse next time he comes knocking to see if *that* encourages him to leave as quickly as a cat!

Though there have been a couple of other wealthy people that have given money away in a similar way to how I give mine away. You may have read the story from a few years ago of the millionaire businessman nicknamed 'Mr Lucky' who a reporter from the Daily Telegraph spent the day with in London whilst he gave random people £1,000 each. Like myself he didn't want his real identity to be revealed so the press gave him the name 'Mr Lucky' because when he stopped someone and gave them the money (or a card as it were informing them how to get it) he used to tell them that it was their lucky day but their luck came with a responsibility and they had to promise to do something good with the money. At the time he'd already given away over £100,000 and on the day the reporter was with him he gave away a further ten thousand and was planning on giving away more. Then there was a guy in America who did the same thing and handed out envelopes containing ten $100 dollar bills. Though unlike myself and 'Mr Lucky' he didn't mind the attention. In fact you could say he courted the attention because he had a camera crew with him from a T.V. station who filmed him doing it. They showed it on live television too and broadcast people's reactions when he gave them the envelopes and they opened them and saw that he'd given them a thousand dollars. And judging by some of the reactions I've seen when *I've* given people money myself I bet it made pretty good viewing!

That guy who did it is now famous in America. Perhaps that was the reason why he did it, to get himself known and become some kind of celebrity. And quite possibly if I'd have approached the BBC or Channel 4 they'd have done a similar thing with me. But I *don't want* to become some kind of celebrity or get myself known. I'd rather remain *un*known, hence using the pseudonym Tom Jones.

And so as the two examples above show, wealthy people randomly giving their own money away isn't unheard of. It's rare but it's not unheard of. Or as the *real* Tom Jones might say, It's Not Unusual! (I knew that pun I thought of as I was driving through Pontypridd would fit in nicely somewhere.)

Chapter Three Can You Spare a Multimillionaire A Pound Please?

As I mentioned, at first I started off by just giving it away at £100 a time. I say 'just' £100 but it's not bad if someone walked up to you and gave you a hundred quid and said, "Here, this is for you," and then walked off. Although the first time I did it I didn't just 'give' it to people – they had to pass a test first.

One of the ideas that one of my friends came up with when we were discussing different ways of how to give my money away was to test people's honesty or generosity in some kind of way. And if they passed the test, reward them by giving them money. I was thinking of different ways of how I could do this and one day when I went shopping with my wife I was stood by the ticket machine on a pay and display car park at a shopping centre waiting to get a ticket for my car. As I was waiting, the person in front of me who was buying a ticket was having a problem putting his money in the machine. And every time he put his pound coin in, the machine wouldn't take it. Then after muttering, "For fuck's sake," several times under his breath, which made me chuckle, he turned around and asked if I had change for a pound or if I had another pound coin I could swap for the one the machine wouldn't take. I said I'd take a look for him and took some change out of my pocket and I saw that I had a couple of pound coins. So I swapped one for his. He said thanks and got his ticket and walked back to his car. Immediately, I had an idea and I turned to my wife who was stood next to me and I said, "That's it!" She asked what I was referring to and I said, "That can be the test."

My wife knew all about my plan to give money away and how in the first instance I planned on testing people's honesty and generosity and then rewarding them if they 'passed' the test. So I explained that what I'd do was, I'd stand by a machine in a pay and display car park and when someone approached I'd ask them if they had a pound. But I wouldn't ask them if they had a pound that they could swap like I'd just done for that bloke or if they had *change* for a pound, such as two fifty pence pieces, instead, I'd just ask them for a pound and make up some excuse that I'd come out without any money or that I'd forgotten my wallet, and if they said yes and gave me a pound to get a ticket I'd give them a £100 in return. My wife said that she thought it was a good idea and so that's what I started doing. However on the day I first did it I had another idea that I thought would test people's generosity further still.

The following week I drove to the same car park. It was a Tuesday morning and it was relatively quiet which was how I was hoping it'd be. I thought it was better to do it on a week day rather than a Saturday or a Sunday as there'd be less people around and I didn't want there to be six or seven people stood at the machine queuing for a ticket when I did it. I just wanted there to be one person by their self if it was possible. It's not that I'm shy or I get embarrassed easily or anything like that. It was more from the *other* person's point of view. I think that sometimes people tend to be more themselves when they're alone than they are in front of a crowd of people. And that's what I wanted. Someone who was being their self and who was genuinely kind by nature and would give me a pound because they *wanted* to rather than feeling they *had* to give me a pound because they were too embarrassed to say no because people were watching.

Originally I was just going to stand by the machine and ask someone for a pound and see what reaction I got. But as I was driving to the car park that morning I thought that a better idea would be to park my car next to the machine and see what reaction I got when I asked someone if they could spare me a pound and they saw that I drove a £150,000 Bentley Continental!

I got there fairly early. There were a few cars already parked on there but I managed to park right next to the machine and I sat there and waited. About ten minutes later a small Peugeot pulled onto the car park driven by a woman who I'd say was in her mid fifties, and she parked up and got out and walked over to the ticket machine and put her money in it. And as she did so I got out of my car and walked towards to her and said,

"Excuse me. You haven't got a pound have you? Only I've come out without my wallet and I've got no change for a ticket." She looked at me and then looked at my car and asked if it was mine and when I said that it was she made a kind of tutting come huffing noise, if you know what mean, and threw her eyes in the air as if to say, 'You cheeky twat! You drive a car like that and you're asking me for a quid!" And she turned and walked back to her car shaking her head as though she couldn't believe I'd had the nerve to ask her for a pound when it was obvious I wasn't short of a few bob.

The second person I asked was also a woman

and I asked her the same thing, if she had a pound for parking as I'd left the house without my wallet. She too noticed my car but unlike the previous woman it didn't seem to be an issue that I'd asked her for a quid even though I drove a top of the range Bentley and that I was clearly a wealthy person. She just said, "I might have. I'll have a look for you," and took out her purse from her handbag and looked through it. She then said,

"You're in luck," and smiled and took out two fifty pence pieces and handed them to me. I thought to myself 'It's not *me* that's in luck it's *you* because you're going to get a hundred quid!' But as she went to give them to me with one hand she held her other hand out for *me* to give *her* something, such as a pound coin or five twenty pence pieces. She must have misunderstood what I'd said so I said to her, "Oh, I'm sorry. I didn't mean have you got *change* for a pound. I meant have you got a pound you could *give* me?" And after I'd said it she looked at me the same way the first woman did, as if I was incredibly cheeky for asking, and her tone changed completely and she said, "No, sorry. I haven't," and put the two fifty pence pieces back in her purse, got her own ticket and walked away.

So on reflection, in the case of the first woman

it came across that the fact I drove an expensive car was the reason that the she wouldn't give me a pound. Maybe if I was driving an old Ford Escort or a transit van she would have given it to me and my gut feeling was that she would have done. But that was the whole point of using the Bentley, to see how people would react when a rich person asked them for a quid and whether it would sway their decision if they gave it or not, and in her case it did. Whereas in the case of the second woman, even though she misheard me at first, I got the impression that the fact I drove an expensive car and that I was obviously wealthy was irrelevant and that she just wasn't the sort of person that would help someone out by giving them a pound to buy a ticket for parking. And from her standpoint I *may as well have been* driving an old Ford Escort or a transit van and she *still* wouldn't have given me a pound to get a ticket. So even though she was very pleasant she wasn't very kind hearted.

The third person I asked however was both very pleasant and very kind hearted and he *did* give me a pound to buy a ticket. He had a good sense of humour too and he took the mickey out of me a little bit. I also got the feeling that not only could I have asked him for a pound like I did when he was on his own and he'd have given it to me, I could have asked him for a pound in front of a crowd of people (that as for the reasons I explained I didn't want to do) and he would've still have given it to me simply because it was in his nature to do something like that rather than give it because he might have been too embarrassed to say no. In fact, I got the impression that I could have asked him anything at all in front of a crowd of people, including questions about his sex life and he'd have answered openly and honestly and not been embarrassed one bit!

I was sat in my car with the door open and a BMW pulled into the car park and parked more or less opposite me, and this bloke got out and walked over to the machine. He looked like an 'ordinary' type bloke. He was about forty five years old and he was wearing shorts and a T shirt. He was quite a biggish bloke and he looked like he'd just come out of the gym. His BM' was a 3 series model which was around eight years old and I noticed it had one or two scrapes above the wheel arch and the alloys looked a bit scuffed. It was far from an old banger but it wasn't in pristine condition either.

The reason for describing him and his car in such detail is to paint a picture for you of how he came across. If I just described him as a middle aged man driving a BMW an image may come into your head of a well-to-do, smartly dressed business executive who was driving a brand new top of the range model. But this guy wasn't like that at all. I know they say you should never judge a book by its cover - and I never do - but he was far from the business executive type.

As he was getting his money out of his pocket I got out of my car and he looked over at me and said, "Alright mate."

So I replied, "Yes, I'm fine thanks," and then said, "You couldn't do me a favour could you?"

He said, "What's that?"

And so I said, "You haven't got a pound I could have, have you? Only I've left my wallet at home and I've got no change for a ticket." He smirked and gave a little laugh, glanced at my car and said,

"Are you taking the piss! You drive a car like that and you're tapping a fucking quid off me!" I gave a little laugh myself and replied, "I don't normally do it. I just realised when I parked up that I didn't have any money."

Well I wasn't *completely* lying was I? I did have money on me but I don't normally ask people in car parks for a quid - it was my first day. Albeit the *third time* that day. Or rather the third time in the space of fifteen minutes!

He then said, "I'm only joking. Here you go," and gave me a £1 coin. I said, "That's very kind of you," and he smiled and replied 'no problem' and turned to walk back to his car. And as he started to walk off I said to him, "Oh, before you go, this is for you," and when he turned around I took two fifty pound notes out of my pocket and walked over to him and handed them to him along with the pound coin he'd just given me.

He looked slightly bemused, as you'd expect if you gave someone a pound and they gave you £101 straight back! And he said, "What's that for?" I didn't tell him the full story of what I was doing, obviously, I just said that I wanted to thank him for his kindness and for helping me out. And I told him about the two women I'd asked before him who'd refused and that I thought it was very kind of him to give me a pound even though it was obvious I was quite wealthy, or *very* wealthy as it were.

He wasn't totally convinced with the reason I gave him for me doing it I must admit. And he laughed and started looking around and asked me where the cameras were hidden because he thought it was a prank for one of those wind up programmes you see on television. So I assured him it wasn't a prank. I also assured him that the two £50 notes I'd just given him weren't fakes either as he was holding one of them up to the light to check if it was real! I then thanked him once again for his generosity and jokingly said that he might want to put the hundred pounds towards sorting the scratched paint work out above the wheel arch on his car. I then wished him a good day, got in my car and drove off. And that was the first time I ever gave money to a total stranger.

I've given money away like that many times since on car parks and I still do it now every so often, though not so much as a test like the first few times I did it. And rather than ask for a pound I just pretend to be ten or twenty pence short. It's surprising how many people won't think twice about giving someone ten pence but they're slightly more reluctant to part with a quid. And rather than park my car next to the machine I now park it across the other side of the car park so it's out of sight from the people I ask. I found that the only problem with letting people see I drive a £150,000 car is that they become very judgemental and more often than not they refuse to give me any change which in turn means *I* can't give *them* £100. This defeats the object somewhat of what I'm trying to do - give money away - as I end up going home with most of the £50 notes that I took out to give away!

I've also come up with a new way of giving money to people in car parks which is a bit more fun. Fun for *me* that is! It's a variation on the way I've described above only I don't hand the money to people personally.

I bought a load of penalty charge notice envelopes off eBay. You'll know the sort I mean. They're yellow with black writing on them and they look identical to the ones traffic wardens stick on your windscreen if you're illegally parked in say a residents parking zone or if you've parked your car on double yellow lines. Or in my case when I was once issued with a parking ticket, with about an inch of my back wheel parked on a double yellow line. This just goes to show that not only can some people whom you ask for a quid in a car park be judgemental if they see that you own a very expensive car, so too are some traffic wardens.

These types of envelopes are also used by some private companies that run pay and display car parks and when they issue a ticket they'll put the ticket inside the envelope and stick it on your windscreen or put it under your wiper. And what I do is, I'll ask someone who's buying a ticket at the machine if they can spare twenty pence and if they give it to me I'll just thank them but I won't give them the £100. I'll then wait until they've put the ticket they've just bought in their car and once they've left the car park I'll walk over to their car and leave a 'penalty charge notice' under their windscreen wiper with the £100 inside it along with the 20p they've given me and a note saying 'thank you' on it. The only difference between doing it this way and the other way is that I don't get to see the reactions and the looks of bewilderment on the faces of the people who I'm giving the money too. Well, not often anyway.

I've only ever seen one person's reaction to this as normally I've long gone by the time they return to their car. And this bloke's reaction was hysterically funny. The bloke was hysterical too, only not with laughter.

It was on a multi storey car park and I'd asked this guy for twenty pence and he gave it to me without hesitation so when he'd left the car park I put one of the penalty charge notice envelopes with two £50 notes in it under his windscreen wiper. But as I put it under the wiper I noticed a car park attendant walking around checking the cars making sure people had bought a ticket. So I quickly put the wiper back down with the black and yellow envelope under it and walked back to my car and got in it. But then as I was about to drive off I looked across the car park and saw that the bloke who'd given me the twenty pence was walking back towards his car which now had a 'penalty charge notice' stuck on the windscreen. He must have forgotten something as it was no more than two or three minutes since he'd left. And to make matters worse, or better depending on which way you look at it and depending on your sense of humour, the car park attendant was now only four or five cars away from this bloke's car. So I wound my window down (and sunk in my seat!) and when the bloke got about ten feet from his car he saw the penalty notice under his wiper. And he turned and screamed at the parking attendant,

"What the fuck have you give me that for? I've got a fucking ticket you blind bastard!" And he stormed over to his car, ripped the penalty charge notice envelope from under the windscreen wiper, marched up to the parking attendant and rammed it in his chest. I thought, 'Oops! Time for a sharp exit,' and drove off.

As I was driving away I looked in my rear view mirror and I could see the attendant trying to calm the bloke down and motioning with his hands trying to explain that he hadn't issued the ticket. Really, I should've got out of my car and gone and explained everything but it just didn't cross my mind to do so. Possibly because I was too busy laughing! Hopefully they eventually looked inside the envelope, found the £100 along with the twenty pence piece and the thank you note and all ended well.

That one didn't quite go to plan, and on the whole it is a bit of a cruel way of rewarding someone for their act of kindness, but it was quite amusing all the same. I know myself, and probably so too do quite a few of you reading this what it feels like when you walk back to your car and you see that you've been issued with a parking ticket. You feel annoyed even though it has been rightly issued. (And you'd feel *even more* annoyed if the ticket had been issued when your tyre tread was barely touching the yellow paint like mine was.)

So envisage walking back to your car and you see a yellow and black penalty notice charge envelope stuck on your windscreen that had been *wrongly* issued because you know that you'd bought and displayed a parking ticket. You'd be absolutely fuming. But then when you opened the envelope and found £100 and a thank you note inside instead of a fine you'd be over the moon.

You'd be slightly confused but over the moon! Your emotions would go from one extreme to the other and you'd go from being absolutely furious to being absolutely elated in the space of thirty seconds. And if you saw a traffic warden or a parking attendant near your car you'd feel like giving them a hug and kiss instead of wanting to punch them! And I don't doubt that the people whose cars I left those penalty charge notices on would've had the exact same emotions. So even though it may have been a slightly cruel way of rewarding them I'm sure that in the end they'd have seen the funny side and that they'd have been only too happy to accept their 'fine'.

Chapter Four Acting On An Impulse

Believe it or not I once gave a traffic warden some money. Not as a bribe so he wouldn't give me a ticket but because he did *someone else* a favour by not giving *them* a ticket. Now I appreciate that traffic wardens aren't the most popular of people and that most of you are reeling back in horror thinking, 'he gave away some of his money to a traffic warden! They're the last people you'd give it to.' And I would imagine that most of them don't even get so much as a 'hello' off a member of the public as they walk past them let alone have money given to them. But at the end of the day they're only doing the job that they're paid to do. And I say that even though I know only too well myself that some traffic wardens can be overzealous when it comes to issuing parking tickets. Although when one stuck a ticket on the windscreen of my Bentley because I'd ever so slightly scuffed those double yellow lines, I got the feeling that it wasn't a case of that particular warden being overzealous, he (or she) was just jealous. But you get good and bad in every walk of life and some traffic wardens are worse than others. Some will deliberately go out of their way to issue a ticket whereas others are more lenient. And I thought that the one I gave the money to deserved it because not only was he lenient, he actually went out of his way *not* to issue the ticket. He certainly was one of the 'good 'un's.'

It was about a fortnight or so before Christmas and I was sat in a coffee shop not far from where I live and I saw this traffic warden walking down the high street. The coffee shop was on the corner of the high street and a side street, and the side street had limited parking spaces on one side only which were all taken. This was where I'd parked *my* car so I was okay. And on the opposite side it was all double yellow lines and a car was parked on them, and as the traffic warden walked past the shop and looked down the side street he saw it.

Now probably nearly all traffic wardens would have just issued a ticket there and then without hesitation but this one didn't. He looked up and down the street and then walked a little bit further down it, had a look around and then walked back to the car. He then looked over towards the coffee shop I was in and walked over and opened the door and stepped in and asked if the car belonged to anyone. Everyone in there said it wasn't theirs so he said, "Okay, thanks. I'll try the hairdressers next door."

I thought 'what a nice thing to do.' He could have quite easily, and quite rightly, issued a ticket but he didn't. And not only did he go in the hairdressers next door trying to find the owner, he also went in the shop next door to that. He then crossed over the road and went in the betting shop and the estate agents and then the nail bar next door to it where the lady whose car it was, was having her nails done. And she came out with him and walked over to her car with him.

He'd gone to all that trouble just so he didn't have to issue her with a ticket.

By that time I'd finished my coffee so I got up and left and as I walked past the woman whose car it was I said to her, "You were lucky there weren't you. They're not all like that," and she replied,

"I know! He'll definitely be on my Christmas card list." The traffic warden laughed and said,

"That'll be a first, getting a Christmas card off a member of the public."

So I said to him, "I bet this is a first too," and I took a £20 note out of my pocket and gave it to him and said, "Merry Christmas!" The woman then kissed him on the cheek and said, "Thank you so much," and got in her car and drove off. I then walked away leaving the traffic warden stood there looking completely stunned with a twenty pound note in his hand and lipstick on his cheek!

And if any traffic wardens are reading this or if the traffic warden who I'm referring to happens to be reading this himself, please don't think I discriminate by giving motorists a hundred pounds yet I only give traffic wardens twenty. It's just that that's all the cash I had on me that particular morning!

That's an example of what I was saying earlier about how that on a lot of occasions when I give money away it's on the spur of the moment and that how on some days I go out having no intention of giving money away but end up doing so. And this next one is also a similar example.

Like the first few times I gave money away this too took place on a car park although this time I didn't 'issue' any penalty notice charges. However, I did give away a bit more than the usual one hundred pounds. I gave *two hundred and fifty pounds* away and it was to a nurse. And if anyone deserves a bit more money it's nurses. In actual fact, it's not a *bit* more they should get, they should get a *lot* more.

It was on Tesco's car park and as I was getting back into my car I saw her walking across the car park carrying her shopping bags. I could see she was in a bit of discomfort because she was grimacing as she walked. And she was hobbling but trying to walk upright at the same time as though she was trying to keep her back straight. So as she walked passed, or hobbled passed, I asked her if she wanted a lift with her shopping and she said, "Oh, if you don't mind, thanks," so I took her bags and carried them to her car for her. I asked her what the problem was and she said that she'd pulled her back lifting a patient out of bed the day before and that it was really painful. So I said to her that when she got home she needed to put her feet up and take it easy for a day or two and she half laughed and said, "I wish I *could* take it easy but I can't afford too, and I'm back in work tomorrow as well!" She then opened her car boot and I put her bags in for her and she said thanks again. And as she went to open her car door I took my wallet out of my pocket and took five fifty pound notes out of it and said to her, "Here, phone in sick in the morning," and handed them to her.

She looked at me with a look that I got used to seeing over time - a very puzzled one - and said, "What?!!"

So I just said, "Take tomorrow off and rest your back," and gave her a little wink, put the £250 in her hand and walked back to my car and drove home.

Something I learnt to do quite quickly when I started to give money to people was to walk away as soon as I'd handed it to them before they had the chance to say anything and ask why I'd done it so as to avoid getting drawn into giving an explanation. Though many a time when I gave a person money they were too shocked to speak anyway and they just stood there speechless like this next woman did.

It happened in the same Tesco's where I gave the nurse the £250 only this time it wasn't on the car park but at the checkout. And again it was one of those occasions where I hadn't gone out with the intention of giving money away but ended up doing so. I had no intention of going out at all actually that evening and only went out because my wife had asked me if I'd go and get her something from the chemist. And like I did with the nurse, I gave this woman the money so she too could take the day off work, or the *night* as it was.

It was early evening and I'd just uncorked a bottle of wine and I was about to have a glass of it. I asked my wife if she wanted one herself and she said that she didn't, which I thought a bit unusual as she normally does. She's not an old wino by any stretch of the imagination but she does like the odd glass of Chateau Lynch Moussas now and then, as do I.

She kept getting up and down out of the armchair and walking around and then sitting back down again, and she had a slightly agitated look on her face. And then she asked me if I'd nip out and get her something from the chemist. I suddenly came over in a cold sweat because with her not wanting a glass of wine, coupled with looking anxious and agitated and pacing up and down the room, and then asking me to go to the chemist for her, I was dreading to ask what it was she wanted in case she said it was a pregnancy test kit! Luckily it wasn't. And thank god for that. The four I've already got cost me a small fortune as it is. And with first class seats costing anything up to £10,000 each on a flight, I may well have to start putting *my own* kids in economy class whenever we go on holiday if a fifth one came along!

My wife said that the nearest chemist was in Tesco's so I put the cork back in the bottle of wine and drove down there to get what she wanted. I went in and got them and as I was at the self service checkout paying for them there was a woman paying for her shopping at the till next to me and she was sneezing and coughing and snivelling as she was doing so. She looked awful. I don't mean she was ugly. She was quite attractive as it happens! I mean she didn't look well. She looked like she had the flu or a very heavy cold at least. So I made a bit of a joke and said to her that I hoped she'd bought some Lemsip, and she smiled, sneezed, and held up two boxes of them! So I said, "You want to take *them* and go straight to bed."

And she replied, "Bed? You're joking aren't you? I've got to go to work in an hour!"

I said to her that she shouldn't have to go into work when she was like that surely, and she said that she had no choice because she wouldn't get paid if she didn't. (Whatever happened to statutory sick pay?) So after I paid for the item's that my wife was in desperate need of, I took £100 out of my pocket and said to the woman, "Here you go. You can take the night off now," and gave it to her and walked off without giving her the chance to say anything. Not that she *could've* said too much because she was too busy coughing and sneezing! And as I walked past outside I glanced through the big glass window and saw her just standing there staring at me as if she'd been struck dumb, not quite believing what had just happened to her.

I then went back home, gave my wife the things she'd sent me out to get for her, took the cork back out of the bottle of wine, poured myself a glassful and sat down comfortably in the armchair and enjoyed the rest of the evening. And after my wife had applied the Hemorrhoid cream and inserted one of the suppositories that I'd just been out to get for her, she too sat down - albeit slightly *less* comfortably - and *tried* to enjoy the rest of the evening! (She'll kill me for putting that in.)

And considering that that particular money giveaway and the one involving the nurse both took place at Tesco's, I suppose the moral of those two stories could be 'Every Little Helps!'

Tesco's customers aren't the only supermarket customers to have benefited from me giving money away, Sainsbury's customers have benefited too, although it wasn't in the actual store itself or on the car park but in their petrol station next door. And similar to the two ladies in Tesco's, I hadn't planned on giving money away on that day either and I just acted on impulse. But on this occasion it wasn't me that did the deed, it was the cashier.

I was putting some petrol in my car and there was a bloke on the pump on the other side of mine filling his up too and as he was doing it he looked over at me and quipped, "It's not cheap is it!" So I said to him, "It certainly isn't, no." And at around £1.30 a litre he wasn't wrong either!

I finished filling my car up and went in to pay and as I got my money out I looked over and saw that the bloke I was talking to was still filling his up and I noticed his pump number was No.8. So I gave the woman behind the counter the £30.01 for mine (I hate it when I go over by a penny, don't you. No matter how hard I try I always do it) and then I gave her another £50 and said that I was paying for the bloke's petrol on pump number eight as well and said that if it was any less to give him the change. She didn't think anything of it and just said, "Okay," which I thought was a bit odd of her actually as I thought she may have asked why I was paying for it as it can't be everyday someone offers to pay for someone else's petrol as well as their own - even more so considering the bloody price of it! But anyway, she didn't question why and I walked back to my car and got in it and as I pulled away I wound the window down and said to the bloke, "The petrol's not as expensive as you think in here," and I drove off!

I'll never know how much his petrol cost but for arguments sake let's say he filled up the same amount as I did, £30 (and a penny) and when he went in to pay, instead of *him* handing the cashier money, *she* gave *him* twenty quid and told him his petrol was paid for as well! And probably like one or two others I've given money to, this bloke must also have thought it was some kind of wind up. And even if it *would have been* some kind of wind up I'm pretty sure that he wouldn't have minded. I don't think *anyone* would object to being wound up like that if it meant that every time they went to a petrol station and filled their car up they got it for free plus a twenty pound cash back. Though most would probably just get *£19.99* cash back because they've gone over by a penny like I always do!

By all accounts, Mario Balotelli, the former Manchester City and Liverpool footballer did the same thing at a petrol station in Manchester. Only he went one better and paid for the petrol for *everyone* who was filling up their cars at the time. And despite the fact he could well afford it as he was reportedly earning around £120,000 a week, it was still a very generous thing for him to do. And similarly to me paying for that bloke's petrol at Sainsbury's, Mario Balotelli would've been acting on impulse too.

On nearly all the occasions I've given money away it's been on impulse. Having said that, you could argue that I *can't* be acting on impulse because I knew I was going to give it away at some point in one way or another, and if you know you're going to do something then you can't be acting on impulse can you. But what I mean is, even though I may leave my house one morning with the intention of giving money to people I don't actually know who I'm going to give it *to*. So although I do know I'm going to give it to someone I've got absolutely no idea who that person will be.

Take the nurse at Tesco's for example. I didn't wake up that morning and think, 'I'm going to give £250 to a nurse today,' I just happened to see her walking across the car park, helped her with her bags, found out she'd hurt her back and gave her the money so she could have a couple of days off work. On any other day the same nurse might have walked past me carrying her shopping with nothing wrong with her back and I may have just let her walk straight by without saying a word. Then again I might have thought, 'Oh look, there's a nurse. They do a great job. I think I'll give her £250' and give her the money. So most of the time I really don't have any idea at all who, where or when I'll be giving money to. But then there are times when I know *exactly* who I'll be giving it to.

Chapter Five Did Worzel Gummidge Just Pay For My Lunch?

When me and my friends were thinking of ways of how to give my money away, as you know, one of them suggested that rather than give a lump sum of £10,000 to a homeless charity we should give it directly to the homeless people themselves, which we ended up doing. And it was during the course of doing this that I had an idea that I thought would not only repay someone's kindness but would also be quite funny.

Where I live (on the Outer Hebrides for anyone reading that may be thinking of tracking me down and waiting outside my house one morning and mugging me as I leave with a few grand in my pocket to give away) you don't get many people sleeping rough. So me and my friends went into London and handed out £50 notes to all the homeless people we saw. All six of us went and we paired into three groups and went in different directions and we gave each homeless person we saw two notes each. I had £2,000 and I gave the others £2,000 each to give away as well.

I didn't realise it would be so easy and take so little time to give away £12,000 to homeless people in London. And any mathematicians amongst you will have already worked out that we only needed to find a hundred and twenty people who were sleeping rough and give them £100 each to get rid of the twelve grand we had with us. And in hindsight if we'd have Googled just how many people are homeless in London we'd have realised that A, it'd take very little time indeed to find one hundred and twenty people to give £100 each to. And B, we should've taken considerably more money to give to the others. That's because there are currently around seven and a half thousand homeless people living on the streets of London, which is quite staggering, and quite sad. Actually, that figure is a lot higher.

The figure of seven and a half thousand relates to those who are sleeping rough. But there's a difference between being a rough sleeper and being homeless as it's possible to be homeless even though you may not be sleeping rough. For example, someone can be homeless if they're staying in temporary accommodation but they're not rough sleeping because they have a roof over their head at night. So that figure of seven and a half thousand refers only to those who sleep rough on the actual streets, in shop doorways and wherever else they can find shelter. The figure for people that are classed as homeless in London is much higher.

Quite a few of the homeless/rough sleepers we gave the money to didn't even realise we'd given it to them as a lot of them were fast asleep under blankets even though it was daytime. So we just put the money in their pocket, which is probably a much better way of giving it to them when you think about it as it'd be a nice surprise for them when they awake. And the look on their faces when they wake up and put their hand in their pocket and find two fifty pound notes in it would be one to photograph, frame and keep!

Others were sat there with their heads down with a plastic cup in front of them so we just folded the notes up as small as we could and put them in the cup and covered them up with whatever small change was in there so that nobody could see it as they walked passed and take it, which no doubt some unscrupulous people would have done. Although quite a few were awake but again we just folded the notes up and put them in their hand and walked off, and by the time they'd realised how much we'd given them we'd have disappeared around the corner. However one bloke realised immediately how much one of my friends had just given him and got up and ran after him and gave him a big bear hug and said, "Thank You, Thank You, Thank You!" And then told passers-by and people who were stood watching what my friend had done and they all started clapping him! And being the show off that he is he gave the crowd that had gathered around a little bow followed by a tip of his hat (even though he wasn't wearing one) milked the applause and then casually strode off. I wouldn't have minded so much but it was my money he was giving away!

When he told us what had happened we all thought it was hilarious and that's when I got the idea that I thought would be quite funny. And the idea was to pretend to be a rough sleeper and when someone gave me some change I'd give them £100.

So all I did was not have a shave for a few days, got an old jacket from out of the garage that I used to wear when I did a bit of gardening or a bit of DIY. (My wife will laugh when she reads that part because my DIY capabilities are limited to say the least and we also pay a gardener who comes once a fortnight, but I do pull the odd weed or two now and then.) And I got a pair of jeans and dirtied them a little and scuffed up a pair of old shoes. Then on the day, I roughed up my hair, tied a bit of string around my jacket and went and sat in an empty shop doorway in the town centre not a million miles away from where I live. I think I may have gone a bit over the top actually because when I caught a glimpse of myself in the shop window I thought Worzel Gummidge was staring back at me! I looked more like Worzel Gummidge than Worzel Gummidge looked like Worzel Gummidge! Even Aunt Sally would've been hard pushed to tell us apart.

So I sat down in the doorway and put a plastic cup in front of me and waited for someone to give me a bit of change - and I waited, and I waited and I waited. And then I waited some more. And it was whilst I was waiting that I realised just how disheartening it must be for someone who *genuinely* sits in a shop doorway everyday in the hope that someone will give them a bit of change. And it must have been at least two hours - in which time two or three hundred people must have walked past me - before a young woman walked past with her friend. And she stopped, took out her purse, took £1.50 from it and put it in the cup. So I thanked her and she smiled and walked on.

The idea I had in my head that I was going to do was to get up, walk up behind her, tap her on the shoulder and when she turned around give her back the £1.50 she gave me plus £100 and say, 'have a nice day' or whatever came out, and walk away. But as I got up I saw that she was walking towards a bistro opposite. It was quite a posh bistro too that I'd been in myself, and her and her friend went in and sat down towards the back of it. I thought 'this is even better!' So I took the £1.50 out of the cup and stood up and walked over to it.

It was only a fairly small place and the woman that had given me the money was sat side on to the entrance and her friend was sat facing it. And as I opened the door and walked in her friend saw me and nudged the woman and said something to her and nodded towards the door and the woman looked up and saw me walking towards her, and she looked absolutely horrified! God knows what must have been going through her mind as I walked towards her table. She was either thinking that I was going to ask her for more money or say 'is that all you've given me you tight cow!'

It was really busy in there as well, and it was one of those moments where everyone seemed to stop talking at the same time and the room fell silent, and they all stared at me. And I walked up to her and put the £1.50 she'd given me on the table. I then took five twenty pound notes out of my pocket and put them down next to it and said,

"Have lunch on me!" She looked very confused to say the least. She also looked very relieved! And you could tell by the look on her and her friend's face - and *everyone else's* face in there - that they were thinking, 'Hang on a minute. Worzel was sat in that shop doorway opposite a minute ago asking people for spare change and now he's just walked in and bought lunch for someone he doesn't even know!"

It's not just lunch I've bought for people I don't know. I once bought everyone in the queue at a kiosk in the Lake District an ice cream who I didn't know either.

We were there for a few days and it was a lovely sunny day so I got an ice cream for me, my wife and the kids. I got my money out to pay for ours and on impulse again, I had a look at how many people were behind me in the queue and saw that there were about thirty mums, dads and kids. So I had a quick tot up and gave the woman £17 for ours and then gave her another £70 and told her to give everyone behind me an ice cream. And even though it only equated to around £2.50 per person, which is by far the smallest amount I've ever given to someone, I'm sure it was still much appreciated by all the mum's and dad's.

When I ordered the ice creams for me, my wife and my kids I asked the lady who was serving what flavours she had and she replied, "I've got vanilla, chocolate, strawberry, or mango," and she wheezed as she spoke and patted her chest and seemed unable to continue speaking. So I said to her, "Have you got laryngitis or emphysema?" and she said, "No, I've just told you. I've only got vanilla, chocolate, strawberry, or mango!"

If you think about it, that lady who sells the ice cream in the Lake District gives more away in a day than I do. I only give a few hundred or maybe a thousand away in a day but she gives *hundreds and thousands* away a day! But enough of my (bad) ice cream jokes and let's get back to me giving away some of my *hundreds of millions*.

On the same day, less than twenty feet away from that ice cream kiosk at Lake Windermere, two other parents also appreciated one of my smaller giveaways after I paid for their boat hire.

We were just walking back down the jetty after going out on the lake on one of those small motorised boats when I heard this young lad who was around ten years old ask his mum and dad if they could hire one. I heard his dad say that he couldn't afford it as it was too dear (even I thought it was a bit on the expensive side at nearly £40 an hour) and I heard his son say, "Oh please Dad. It'll be fun." Now I'm sure if his dad would've had the money he'd have hired one of the boats and I'm also fairly sure he would have been feeling a bit gutted for his son that he couldn't afford to take him out on one. So as I walked past the boat hire office I bought another family ticket and when I turned around his son was down near the edge of the lake throwing stones in the water and his mum and dad were watching him about ten or fifteen feet away. So I walked up to them and said,

"Excuse me. I hope you don't mind. Only I overheard your son asking you if you could hire a boat and you said that you couldn't afford it. So I've bought you a ticket." And I gave it him and said for him to tell his son that he was only kidding when he said he couldn't afford it and that *he'd* bought the ticket and not me. I got the usual bemused looked and he just said, "Oh, erm, right." I think he was momentarily stunned as well as bemused! Then all of a sudden his facial expression changed from bemusement to delight and he said, "Wow! That's brilliant! Thanks very much." His wife was equally bemused and then equally grateful, and as we walked away she shouted to her son, "Michael. Look what your dad's bought." And her son went over to his mum and dad and we - and the rest of Lake Windermere - heard a very loud, "Yesss!"

Sometimes, particularly in situations like that, you have to be careful how you say things. I know not many people are going to take offence when you do something nice for them or pay for something for them such as in situations like that. But some people may look at it as if you're taking pity on them. Some people are very proud, particularly men or dad's and they may well take offence at having something paid for by someone, even more so having it paid for by a total stranger knowing they can't afford it themselves. And they may not like the idea of someone thinking they're some kind of 'charity case.' That's why I gave the ticket to the dad whilst his son wasn't looking. That way, which was the reason why I did it, was so it looked like the dad had bought the ticket. Therefore his son would've thought what a great dad he had. Also, if the son would've been stood with them when I gave him the ticket their reaction might well have been different. His son's reaction wouldn't have been different. He would've still been overjoyed and he would've still deafened everybody on Lake Windermere with a yell of 'Yesss!' But his mum and dad might have been slightly embarrassed, you never know. That's why if I pay for something or give money away and it involves kids I always do it in a way so the mum, dad or both get the credit.

There's also one other parent I know of whose two kids probably shouted 'Yesss!' even louder than young Michael did when they found out where they were going. And I reckon the parent herself was just as happy as her kids. More so actually, and not just because she was happy that I'd paid for them to go on holiday, but also because of the situation she was in that I'd helped her get out of. And apart from the £100,000 I gave to each of my five friends this one was the largest amount I'd given away at the time. It's also without doubt one of the ones that has given me the most pleasure.

Chapter Six The Fairy Godfather

Unlike everyone else I've given money to I did kind of know this person albeit through the friend of a friend kind of thing. There's a bit of a sad story behind it too which I won't go into. It's also one of those that where rather than just give the money away randomly to *anyone*, it went to someone who needed it.

Miss 'X' as I'll refer to her as lived on her own with her two young kids and she'd been through a really tough time. And I mean a *really* tough time, both personally and financially. And knowing what she's been through I wouldn't be surprised if it affected her mentally for a while too. As I say, I got to know of her through a friend of a friend who just happened to be one of the dozen or so who knew about me giving money away and he told me of what had happened and asked if I could help in some way and I said that I would. So I went with him to see her.

At the time she had no idea who I was let alone about me giving money away. All my friend had said to her was that I might be able to help her in some way because of the contacts I had and people I knew. Now however she *does* know who I am and she knows all about the money I give away. As a matter of fact she's probably the only person who knows down to the pound exactly *how much* I've given away to date. Even I don't know the exact figure!

Her main worry was that she'd fallen behind with her rent and hadn't paid it in months and she was on the brink of being evicted from her home. I asked her how much she owed and she said it was over £3,000, so I asked her for the name of her letting agent. And when she told me it just so happened I knew them very well through my dealings in the property market. So whilst she was sat there with me I gave them a call. I told them who I was and what it was regarding and I asked them that if the arrears were paid in full would they halt the eviction proceedings and they said they would. So I said I'd be in the following morning to pay it. I don't think she could quite believe what she'd just heard me say and she didn't speak. She too like the sneezing woman in Tesco had been struck dumb! And although no *words* came out of her, tears did. She just burst out crying and couldn't stop. It must have been such a relief for her knowing she wasn't going to be evicted. The thought of having nowhere for her and her two kids to live must have been causing her to have nightmares - *horrendous* nightmares at that considering what she'd already been through.

When she'd calmed down and composed herself she thanked me and asked how I wanted her to pay the money back. The only problem she said, was that she wasn't working. I told her not to worry about it and I'd sort something out.

She was still a bit tearful and whilst we were sat there chatting her two kids came in the room, two little girls aged five and six, and when they saw that their mum was upset they went over to her and gave her a cuddle and said "Don't worry Mummy. It'll be alright," and she burst into tears again. It was very emotional. It was that emotional I nearly started crying myself!

The two girls were both dressed in Disney princess outfits so I asked them which princesses they were and one of them said that she was Elsa from Frozen and the other said she was Mulan, whoever that was! I'd heard of Elsa, she's the one that sings that annoying 'Let It Go' song from the film, but I can't say I've ever heard of Mulan before. I told them that they both looked like *real* princesses and they said that their mum had told them that she'd take them to Disney World in Florida one day to meet them all.

I think deep down their mum knew that was very unlikely.

Anyway, we chatted for a little while longer and I told Miss X not to worry about things and that I'd be in touch soon and me and my friend left. And the next day I went down to the letting agents and cleared the £3,000 rent arrears for her as promised. I then went home and rang the travel company who I use when we go on holiday and asked them roughly how much a family holiday to Disney World in Florida would cost and she said that it'd be in the region of £6,000 for a decent one staying on the Disney resort itself. So I asked her if she could do some kind of Disney holiday gift voucher for me and charge it to my account and send it to me along with a Disney brochure and she said she would. And when it arrived I went back around to Miss X's house with my friend.

I told my friend what I was planning on doing and that I was also going to tell her all about me giving money away. And as he'd already told me enough about her to know I could trust her not to go telling anyone, I knew it wouldn't be a problem. And knowing what she'd been through I had no qualms whatsoever in helping her the way I did.

So we 'came clean' as it were and told her

everything and I told her that she didn't have to pay the £3,000 back. And just like when I rang the letting agent and said I'd pay the rent arrears it didn't quite sink in and she couldn't believe it. And even though she knew I'd paid them because she'd had confirmation from the letting agent that the arrears had been paid and she was no longer being evicted, she still couldn't believe that I didn't want the money back. And if that wasn't a big enough shock for her, you should've seen her face when I gave her the Disney gift card and brochure and told her to pick a holiday for her and her two 'princesses.' Stunned, bemused, bewildered, gobsmacked, flabbergasted, *bewitched*, you name it she was it. She looked at me like I'd just cast a spell on her. She must have thought I was the fairy godmother! Or should that be the fairy god*father*? Who cares - she certainly didn't! And again, like the bloke at Windermere who I gave the boat ticket to when his son wasn't looking, I gave the brochure and gift card to her when her two daughters weren't there so *she* could give it to them so they'd think that their mum had paid for it like she'd promised them she would. And when it all sank in, just like she did when I rang the letting agents to say I'd clear the arrears for her, she burst into tears again. Only this time they were tears of joy. I then gave her some more good news. I offered her a job. And she now works for me doing my accounts which includes keeping tabs on how much money I've given away, hence her knowing down to the pound how much it is. I also gave her a 'few bob' spending money when she went to Disney.

All told, including the rent arrears, the trip to Disney and the spending money, it was in the region of £10,000 I'd given her which was by far the biggest sum I'd given to someone that I didn't know. Up to this point, barring the £250 I gave the nurse on Tesco's car park, I'd only ever given it away at £100 or £200 at a time, and the one's I've told you about are just a few of the very many. It would be impossible to list every one of the occasions that I've given money away and if I *did* tell you about every occasion then this book would be longer than 'War and Peace' - and probably just as boring. Not only that, I've done it that many times now that I can't honestly remember every occasion, and as I've mentioned once or twice already, people's reactions are pretty much the same when I give them the money. And if I was to list all of them it would just become repetitive which is why I've just told you about some of the better one's or those that are funny.

But it was around this time, or shortly after helping Miss X, that I went through a phase of giving larger amounts of money away. I still gave away a hundred or two hundred pounds at a time but I started handing out a *thousand pounds* at a time too. I don't really know why I started doing it at this point, I just did. Perhaps it was because with me seeing how much joy it brought to Miss X by giving her such a large amount it made me want to give similar joy to other people too. Or perhaps in my subconscious I was thinking of 'Mr Lucky' who gave away a thousand pounds at a time, or the guy in America who handed people an envelope with a thousand dollars inside that prompted me to do it. I've really no idea. I just woke up one morning and decided that I'd start giving bigger amounts away.

The only difference in the way I did it to the way I'd been doing already was that instead of me handing it to them and they could see what I was giving them, i.e. notes/money, I put it inside a brown envelope beforehand so they didn't know it was money I was giving them. So perhaps it *was* in my subconscious about the guy in America handing envelopes to people with money inside that prompted me to do it after all. And whereas before I sometimes gave it to someone who had shown an act of kindness, like those on the car park who had given me a pound or twenty pence to get a ticket, I just gave it to totally random people I came across in the street. And instead of saying things like, 'This is for you' or 'Take the day off work' I just said things like, 'I think this is yours' or 'Have you just dropped this?' and I'd give it to them and walk off. I didn't hang around for them to open it or to see their reaction, I just handed them the envelope and walked away as quickly as I could. There was no point in me hanging around anyway because if I'd have asked, 'Is this yours?' or 'Have you dropped this?' and they'd have replied, 'No,' I'd have been stuck with it! And I didn't want to be stuck with it. I wanted to give it away!

The only problem with doing it this way, not that I considered it at the time because I never had any intention of writing a book about what I've done, is that there aren't a great deal of funny or varying stories I can tell you about how I did it as they were all fairly similar. And this part of the book *would* become repetitive if I told you about every one as it'd be the same thing over and over: I walked up to this bloke and said, "Have you dropped this?" gave him an envelope and walked off. I walked up to this woman and said, "Is this yours?" And gave her the envelope and quickly walked away, etc, etc, etc.

So there's no point in me detailing each and every one of them. But in a nut shell, I'd put £1,000 in each of three or four envelopes and take them out and give them to people. Sometimes I did it in London, which is ideal because it's that busy you can just disappear into the crowds. Other times I did it in other parts of the country if say I was away on business or visiting someone. Though there is *one* example of me doing it this way that's worth telling you about as the person's reaction who I gave it to was pretty funny. And it was one of those 'spur of the moment but *not* spur of the moment' moments I told you about that I sometimes have.

I'd been playing golf in Loch Lomond which is one of the most beautiful places I've ever been too. I've been all over the world and visited some fantastic places and seen some marvellous sights but the scenery up there is simply jaw dropping. It really is. And afterwards I drove to Glasgow to meet someone and I stayed overnight in a hotel not far from the town centre, and the following morning I decided to dish out a few 'one thousands.' So I went to the bank and withdrew £3,000, and the cashier gave me three bundles of

£1,000 in twenty pound notes, each bundle having a red paper band around it showing the amount. I then bought some envelopes and put the money inside them and went for a stroll around the town centre.

I gave the first envelope to a middle aged lady and the second envelope to a young bloke, both within the space of ten minutes or so and both times I asked 'is this yours?' and walked off before they had time to answer. Then as I was walking around the shopping district looking for my next 'victim' I noticed a road sweeper walking towards me. He was an oldish bloke who looked like he wasn't far off retirement age and he was whistling 'whistle while you work', the theme tune from Snow White and the Seven Dwarfs as he pushed his litter trolley down the high street whilst picking up bits of paper. Ironically, he looked like one of the dwarfs himself as he had a big red nose and he was only about 5ft tall! He was also happy as in 'Happy' the dwarf. And as he got closer that's when I had one of my 'spur of the moment' ideas to do something even though I'd already planned on doing it. (I'm sure there's a far easier way of writing that so it makes sense but hopefully you know what I mean!)

So as I walked past him I said, "I couldn't put

this in your trolley could I, only I can't seem to find a bin." He must have thought I was blind because there was one about ten yards away! He said, "Aye, nae bother Son, bung it in." So I threw the envelope in his bin and before I walked away I said, "You know that saying, 'where there's muck there's money,' do you reckon it's true?" And he said, "Well if it is, it does nae apply to me because *I've* never fucking found any!" and started laughing. So I said, "Take a look in that envelope. Today might be your lucky day," and winked at him and I walked a bit further on. I then looked back at him and he was just stood there looking at me. So I stopped and gave a little nod towards his litter trolley and he looked at the envelope and then looked back at me, paused for a second, and then virtually dived in his bin!

He grabbed the envelope, ripped it open and pulled out the bundle of twenty pound notes that still had the red paper band around them with '£1,000' written on it. And he turned, and at the top of his voice he shouted up the street to me,

"There's a fucking grand here!"

I replied, "Yes, I know there is - and it's yours," and I wandered off leaving him stood there feeling even more happy than Happy the Dwarf!

Whistle while you work? I bet he whistled every day from that day on until the day he retired.

Another person who was also about retirement age and who also benefited to the tune of around a thousand pounds was the bloke who I bought a sixty inch plasma TV for in Curry's.

As I've said, a lot of the times when I give money away it's just pure spontaneity and this one was probably the most spontaneous of them all. Normally it's the person who I give it to who's surprised but this time I even managed to surprise myself, not to mention my wife who was stood next to me.

I was paying for a laptop we'd just bought for one of the kid's birthdays and an elderly man and his wife were stood at the till next us. They'd just bought this big Samsung television and were about to pay for it and the assistant was asking them if they wanted to buy an extended three year warranty and the bloke replied, "I can just about afford the tele' let alone another three hundred quid on top for an extended warranty," and half laughed and looked at me and shook his head slightly and raised his eyes as if to say 'they always try and flog it you don't they.' Which they always do and it can be quite annoying. And it's even more annoying when they ask you if you want to buy an extended warranty when you've only bought a toaster that cost a fiver! And after the assistant asked him if he wanted it, for some reason I just blurted out to the bloke, "*Take* the warranty. I'll pay for it. And I'll pay for the tele' too."

Both he and the sales assistant must have thought I was joking because the bloke said, "It'd be nice if you did," and the sales assistant just politely smiled at me and continued to serve them and said to the bloke, "Well without the extended warranty that'll be five hundred and ninety nine pounds, please."

So I said, "No, I'm being serious. I'll pay for it," and handed the sales assistant my credit card. The assistant didn't know what to do or whether to take it or not. He just looked at my card and then looked at the old bloke and then they both just stared at me as if I was mental. The bloke's wife then said to me, "Have you won the lottery or something?"

So I just said, "Sort of," and gestured to the sales assistant to take my credit card. The assistant looked at the man and his wife and said, "Are you happy for him to pay for it?"

I'm sure the *sales assistant* was MORE than happy for me to pay for it and was willing the couple to say yes because he was going to get commission for flogging the three years extended warranty!

The man looked at me and said, "Are you sure?"

I said, "Yes, I'm sure." He then looked at my wife, and even though she couldn't quite believe it herself, casually said, "He does it all the time!" To which the bloke replied, "Well in that case. Yes, thank you very much indeed," and I paid for it and we left.

That was a complete rush of blood and I've never done it since. Well not with a credit card anyway. The only problem with doing something like that in a shop is that it can become a bit awkward and it can draw attention which I don't particularly want. When you give cash to someone you can just give it to them and briefly pass comment and walk off, or say nothing at all and disappear never to be seen again. But in a situation like that, using a credit card, you're stuck there until the transaction goes through and even though it only took a few minutes it seemed like an eternity at time. And after the initial rush of blood that prompted me to do it, in the end I couldn't wait to get out of there. And even though she seemed calm and collected, neither could my wife! And in hindsight it really *wasn't* such a good idea because as my wife pointed out afterwards, the credit card had my name on it which is something I'd rather keep a secret between the chosen few.

Chapter Seven Never Look A Gift Horse In The Mouth (but always look inside a newspaper you find on the tube.)

In between buying plasma televisions totalling nearly a thousand pounds for people I've never met before (and totally confusing the person I bought it for into the bargain) and in the process help sales assistants hit their monthly sales targets for flogging extended warranties that half the time are never claimed on and that are a complete waste of money, and giving a thousand pounds to road sweepers proving that sometimes there *really is* money where there's muck, I also continued to give smaller amounts of cash away too. One way of which was to use a cash point, but instead of taking the money out of the machine when it had been dispensed I'd leave it in it so the person behind me or a passer-by could have it.

I'd leave varying amounts. Sometimes I'd leave £100 other times I'd leave £200. I've done this loads of times and believe it or not every time I've done it when I've started to walk off, if there's someone behind me, without fail they've always said, "Excuse me. You've left your money," which I must admit surprised me. Because when I originally had the idea of giving money away like this (it was actually one of my friends ideas, not mine) although I had a feeling that most people would tell me I'd forgotten to take my money, I thought the odd one or two wouldn't say anything and keep it for themselves. And with everyone telling me I'd 'forgotten' it, it certainly restored my faith in human nature. And whenever anyone told me I'd forgotten my money I'd say, "Yes, I know I have. I've left it for you," and they'd say the usual, such as, 'What?' or 'Are you being serious?' And I'd reply, 'Yes. You can have it. It's yours.' Though on one occasion after I'd left £200 in the machine one bloke who still wasn't sure about taking it even after I'd told him he could have it once shouted to me as I walked away, "How do I know it's your money and that you're not using a stolen card?" And when I replied back, "Well if I'd stolen someone's card to pinch their money I wouldn't leave it in the machine would I?" He gave a look as if to say, 'Hmm, well that's true' and took the two hundred quid and put it in his pocket!

Sometimes I do the same thing even if there isn't anybody behind me and I'll just leave the money sticking out of the machine for someone to find. And whoever finds it, good luck to them, they're welcome to it. Although I have often wondered what the reaction of those people who were stood behind me and told me I'd forgotten my money would have been if they came across the money I'd left sticking out of the machine and nobody was around? Would they have kept it or would they have took it into the bank and handed it in? Hopefully anyone who does find my money hanging out of a cash machine *does* keep it and doesn't hand it in to the bank because I want someone to have it. Mind you, it would be rather ironic - and rather amusing - if someone was caught taking it on the bank's CCTV and seen putting it in their pocket and walking off with it and were later arrested for theft by finding!

So never look a gift horse in the mouth. Especially if the horse is a shiny black one and is stood on its back legs and has 'Lloyds Bank' written underneath it!

A similar way I do it is to pretend I've dropped it. I might be walking down the street and I'll let it 'accidentally' fall out of my pocket. I'll fold £100 or £150 up and if I know someone is behind me I'll drop it. But unlike at the cash machine where whenever I walk away and leave money in it and every time I do so the person behind me tells me I've forgotten it, when I drop it on the pavement not always does the person who's walking behind me tell me. Not that I'm *bothered* they don't tell me. And if I were to look around and actually see them picking it up and putting it in their pocket I wouldn't say anything. But it's odd how that at a cash point people never fail to say something but when people see me drop it on the street they're not as honest and don't always say, "Excuse me. You've dropped your money." Quite a few do and when they do I say the same thing I say at the cash point, 'keep it.' Perhaps the reason some people don't say anything is that maybe at the cash machine they feel as if they'd be stealing it from the person who they've just seen withdraw it. But maybe when picking it up off the pavement they feel as if it's more a case of them 'finding' it even though they've seen it fall out of someone's pocket. Or it could just be that those behind me at the cash machine happen to be decent honest people whereas those that pick it up and keep it when they see it fall out of my pocket are just low life thieving bastards with no morals! But however you may class them, they're welcome to it. And anyway, as they say, finders keepers.

Somewhere else I used to deliberately drop money was on the tube in London and not one person ever told me I'd dropped it. But I wasn't expecting anyone to tell me to be honest and for two reasons. One, it's that busy down there that nobody may have even noticed I dropped it. And two, most people on the underground can't even be bothered to say sorry if they've barged into you let alone go out of their way to pick your money up and hand it back to you if they saw you drop it. So I don't do it anymore down there. But what I do still do if I'm travelling on the tube is to put money inside a newspaper, usually the free one, the Metro, that more often than not you get given to you or you can pick up as you enter the station.

Nine times out of ten, someone will always pick up a newspaper if there's one on the seat next to them on the tube and start to read it. So I'll get one as I go in the station and put money inside it and then put it on the seat. Then I'll go and sit a bit further up the carriage or on the seat opposite and wait for someone to sit down and pick it up and start reading it. And it's that busy on the underground it doesn't take long before someone does. And the look on the person's face when they turn the page and eight or nine twenty pound notes fall out is hilarious. You can see them looking downwards towards their lap and they have a quick look either side of them to see if anyone has noticed, perhaps thinking that the paper belongs to the person sat next to them, and then they'll scrunch the notes up in their hand and get off at the next stop. It probably isn't even their stop and it may even make them late for work! But they're not bothered. They just want to get off as quick as they can with the money. But others are more relaxed about it and will just screw the money up in their hand and discretely put it into their pocket or handbag. Then they'll fold the paper up and put it back down where they got it from on the seat next to them and calmly sit there until it *is* their stop. Then they'll casually get up from their seat and get off and walk up the escalator with a rather smug look on their face.

Imagine that happening to you on the tube on your way to work, picking up a free newspaper and finding hundred quid in it. You'd feel like doing back flips up the escalator when you got off never mind standing on it with a smug look on your face as you went up it. And you'd probably feel like doing back flips all the way to work too once you got outside. And I bet some of those people who found the money grabbed every Metro they could as they left the station. Some probably even rang in work sick and then spent the rest of the day travelling the underground getting on and off tubes picking up newspapers that people had left behind!

I used to, and still do things like that on certain days of the week and at certain times too, like on a Monday morning. It's a good time to do it because nearly everyone is cheesed off on a Monday morning because they're going back to work after the weekend and if something like that happens to you on your way to work it'd cheer you up no end and get your week off to a good start. Likewise, if it happened on a Friday afternoon, which is when I sometimes also do it, it's a good time because it'd get your weekend off to a great start if you found a couple of hundred quid on your way home.

Another good time to do things like that, or to just give money to someone, is in the run up to Christmas which I've done for the last couple of years. Though I suppose if you found £150 in the Metro on your way to work on a Monday morning in the middle of July it'd feel pretty much like Christmas had come early. And if someone bought you a £600 tele' in Curry's in October you *really would* think Christmas had come early!

But as I'm sure you know yourselves, Christmas costs a fortune, particularly if you've got kids. So to give someone a few quid in mid December or if they were to find it around that time of year they'd probably appreciate it even more so than they would at any other time of year, like the guy I gave it to on Christmas Eve as I was entering a car park. (I must have a fetish about giving it to people on car parks.) As I drove in, this bloke was leaving and he wound his window down and passed me his ticket and said that there was two hours left on it if I wanted it. I said, "That's great, thanks," and took it. And before he drove off I said to him,

"Here, take this," and took £100 out of my pocket and handed it to him and said, "Merry Christmas!" and then drove into the car park. He was that surprised he stalled his car!

A few weeks before last Christmas one of my friend's suggestions was to dress up as Santa and hand money out which at first I thought wasn't a bad idea. But having thought about it I decided it may not be the best way of doing it as it might have brought too much attention. Word would have soon got around that some guy dressed as Father Christmas was giving money away in the shopping centre and there would've been chaos. The shopkeepers might not have been too happy either as there'd have been no customers in the shops spending money - they'd all have been stood in a queue in front of me holding their hand out! So we ditched that idea and I just carried on doing it the way I had been, giving it to random people. Though similar to when I put the £1,000 inside an envelope before giving it to people, I put the money inside a Christmas card and put the card in an envelope and *then* gave it to people, and wished them a Merry Christmas. Everyone I gave a card to looked a little bit surprised but every one of them (except one) took it and said, "Oh! Thank you," or said, "Merry Christmas to you too," though I never actually saw anyone's reaction when they opened the cards and saw what I'd put inside - £200.

The guy who gave me his car parking ticket on Christmas Eve is probably feeling a little miffed right now if he's reading this and is probably thinking, 'He gave everyone else £200 but he only gave me £100? And I saved him two quid as well!' Sorry pal, but that's all I had on me. I owe you £100!

It's not that I *wanted* to see anyone's reaction after I'd given them the card but the reason I didn't see it was because after they'd taken it and said thanks, rather than open it there and then they just carried on walking with it, which was what I hoped they'd do anyway. That way, I thought it'd be an even better surprise for them when they got home and opened it and found the money. And a lot of the time I deliberately gave it to people who were carrying shopping bags so they *wouldn't* open it there and then. Not that many people are going to put all their bags down when they're rushing around trying to get their Christmas shopping done just to open a card that some odd ball stranger has given them. Though thinking about it now, there was probably no need to deliberately give it to those carrying loads of shopping because even if you were empty handed and someone gave you a Christmas card on the street you wouldn't open it in front of them would you? You'd just politely thank them and take it and open it when you got home. It's probably happened to you yourself when you've been talking to one of your neighbours and they've said,

"Oh, hang on a minute, I've got a card here for you," and they've gone in their house and got it for you. And when they've given it to you, you haven't opened it in front of them (and thought what a crap card that is) you've waited until you've got home and opened it - and *then* thought 'what a crap card that is!' So I probably really needn't had bothered targeting those laden down with bags full of Christmas shopping.

Others I 'targeted' with the Christmas cards were mums who were with their kids. And mums and dads who were coming out of places like Toys R Us or similar shops like the Entertainer, who didn't have their kids with them but who I presumed had been shopping for their kid's presents. And even though when they opened the card and found two hundred quid in it they would have been extremely happy, knowing how much kids toys cost these days, £200 probably just about covered the cost of one present!

But you always get one as the saying goes. And unfortunately for this one he lost out on two hundred smackers.

It was starting to drizzle with rain a little bit so I stood in a doorway next to Waterstones (a place where quite a few avid book readers were also to get a rather nice surprise) and I had just the one card left and this young bloke in his mid twenties walked past. And as he did I offered it to him and said Merry Christmas, and without even turning his head to look at me, he very abruptly said,

"NO!" I thought, 'You ignorant twat. I'm trying to give you a couple of hundred quid here not flog you The Big Issue!'

When I went home and told my wife what had happened she nearly peed herself laughing. And she said that the bloke could probably be forgiven as it wouldn't have been the first time I'd sheltered in a shop doorway like a Big Issue seller waiting for someone to give me a few pence. The cheeky cow also said that there wasn't a great deal of difference between the clothes I had on and my Worzel Gummidge outfit! Needless to say, my five friends also found it highly amusing. None more so than the one who was given a big bear hug in central London by one of my 'Big Issue selling homeless friends' as he put it.

But that young bloke's loss was someone else's gain and I handed it to a lady who passed by next and who took it and said thank you. Manners cost nothing, eh?

Quite a few others also gained at Christmas time. And much like that ignoramus who couldn't even be bothered to look at me, they too didn't see my face. The difference being that where he saw me stood there and deliberately ignored me, these people didn't even see me. That's because I sent the money to them in the post.

Chapter Eight 'All The Postman Ever Brings Is Bills'

The idea to post money to people first came to me earlier in the year well before Christmas although the idea to post it actually came from *another* idea I had that I decided against doing.

I was watching the television one night and that advert came on for the Postcode Lottery, the one where they knock on someone's front door and give them a cheque for whatever amount it is they've won. And at first I thought it would be a good idea to do a similar thing at Christmas time and knock on someone's door and give them a Christmas card with two hundred quid in it. But after thinking about it a bit more I decided it wasn't such a good idea after all as it might be a bit intrusive and a bit *too* forward. It's not too bad giving a card to someone you don't know in the street and wishing them Merry Christmas, even though they may think it's a bit odd. But knocking on someone's front door and doing it may be thought of as VERY odd and quite possibly very worrying. It may be an old lady who lives on her own that answers the door or a kid whose parents are out. And could you imagine what the parents would think if they came home and their young son or daughter told them that some strange man they'd never seen before knocked on the front door and gave them a Christmas card with £200 in it? I think if *I* came home and one of *my* kids said that had happened - not that anyone *can* knock on my front door unless the security gates are opened for them first - rather than think, 'Yippee, £200!' I'd be a little bit worried and I'd be straight on the phone to the police!

So I decided against doing that one and crossed that idea off the list. However a few weeks later I won on the premium bonds and a cheque arrived in the post. "Money goes to money, eh!" you all say. Well, sort of. But it was only £100.

Nonetheless, even though I'm as wealthy as I am it was still a nice feeling when I opened the envelope and saw that I'd won. And that's when it dawned on me how I could do my own version of the postcode lottery without actually knocking on people's front doors. I could just post money to them. And the more I thought about it the more I realised that it would be an even better way of giving money to people than it would handing it out in person like I'd been doing. It'd be a hell of a lot easier too. For a start I wouldn't even have to leave my house to do it. I could just put money in an envelope, address it to someone and stick it in the post box. I'd also be able to give it to people who lived farther afield rather than just giving it to people that live in and around the London area and in the south where I live. (You didn't *really* believe me when I said I lived in the Outer Hebrides did you!)

Also, me opening that envelope and finding a cheque for £100 inside from the Premium Bonds, which was a nice surprise, gave me an idea of how people would feel when they opened the Christmas card I'd sent them and found £200 inside. Sure, they'd be mystified as to who'd sent it but nonetheless it'd be a lovely surprise for them a couple of weeks before Christmas. And if by chance they happened to be in the house at the time and they saw the postman walking down the path it'd be even better, because there's something about the moment you see the postman opening the gate and coming down your path, isn't there? Although *your* postman probably isn't knackered and out of breath by the time he gets to your front door like mine is. That's because it's about a mile and a half walk from the gate to my front door! Postmen must hate delivering to my house. I bet they draw straws at the sorting office to see who cops for it. Mind you I do tip them well at

Christmas. Guess what they get? Correct - a card with £200 in it!

When the postman comes down the path you always get a slight tinge of excitement wondering what he's going to bring you, and when you hear the letter box go no matter what you're doing you stop doing it and go and get the post. Usually the excitement evaporates very quickly and you feel deflated when you realise that all he's brought you is your gas bill. And with energy prices forever increasing these days that's one envelope *nobody* looks forward to opening. Even *I* dread opening that one.

Last winter, (February 2018) when the 'beast from the east' struck, my gas bill was over £600 for the quarter. No, that's not a typo - £600!!! When I opened it and saw how much it was I nearly passed out - as did anyone who visited our house at that time of year. That's because as a result of my wife and kids having the central heating on 24/7 our home was turned into a seven bedroom Swedish sauna! It was like living in an oven. It was that hot I had no need for the greenhouse I've got at the bottom of my garden I just grew my tomatoes in the living room!

Most letters the postman brings have your name and address *printed* on the envelope or you can see your name and address through the 'window' on the envelope. And you automatically know it's just going to be a council tax bill, or a bank statement or your credit card bill. That's another one I dread opening, my credit card bill. And trust me. You really wouldn't want *that one* dropping through your letter box! "I wonder how much his credit card bill usually is?" I hear you ask. Well put it this way. It's not dissimilar to my gas bill only the six is replaced by a one and there's always a couple more nought's on the end!

But when you pick up your post and you see an envelope that's *hand* written, straight away you think, 'I wonder what this is?' And it arouses curiosity and you can't wait to open it. So with all this in mind I started sending out Christmas cards in the post with £200 inside them in hand written envelopes to random addresses up and down the country. In total I sent out nearly two hundred cards with two hundred pounds in each one (£40,000 in total to save you working it out) and I sent them all over the country. All over the UK actually, from Aberdeen to Cornwall and from Swansea to Great Yarmouth and places in between such as Birmingham, Kent, Newcastle, Liverpool, Manchester, North Wales (where my 'caravan' is) Gloucester, and Lincoln.

I sent four or five cards to each town or area and for a bit of amusement for myself I started off at places beginning with 'A' and went through the alphabet trying to think of a town for each letter to send them to: **A**, Aberdeen, **B**, Birmingham, **C**, Carlisle, **D**, Doncaster, and so on, though I must admit I couldn't think of any places beginning with **X** or **Z** to send the cards to. Though I have since been told that there is a village beginning with 'Z' called Zennor which is near St Ives in Cornwall. I'll have to remember that one for next Christmas.

I didn't just put on the envelope 'To any Geordie in Newcastle,' or 'To any Scouser in Liverpool' or 'To any Manc' in Manchester' and then put them in the pillar box. What I did was, I went on Google Earth and 'street view' and got the names of a few streets in each town and then went on Royal Mail's postcode finder and got the postcode for it and addressed it to 'The Homeowner' on whatever the street was named and added the postcode and a house number and did it that way. I also used to zoom in on a house on street view in order to get the house number. Though one thing I didn't do was put 'return to sender' on the back of the envelope because I didn't want the money back! But I did write things like 'Have a lovely Christmas' or 'From your secret

Santa' in the card and then put the two hundred pounds inside it and then put it in the post box.

However not everyone who I first got the address of got the card and the money. That's because I changed my mind and decided not to send it to them. And the reason I changed my mind was because when using Google Street View and I picked up that little yellow man and dragged and dropped him on someone's road, when I zoomed into the houses I saw that some of them were bigger than mine! And I thought, 'Well two hundred quid isn't going to make a great deal of difference to *your* Christmas, mate!' So I picked up the little yellow fella and dropped him a few miles up the road and sent the cards to a street that didn't look quite as up market as the one I'd just been on. And would you believe that whilst looking for somewhere beginning with 'W' to send the cards to, whilst looking in Worcester I dropped the yellow man in a place called Bell End! And being the slightly childish person I am with a silly sense of humour I addressed one of the cards to 'A Bell End' and just put the postcode DY9 underneath it and popped it in the post, which no doubt would have raised a chuckle or two at the Royal Mail's sorting office in Worcester. I wonder which bell end in Worcestershire got the two hundred quid!

Stumbling across 'Bell End' prompted me to Google other places with rude names and amongst others I came across were, *Nob End* in Lanarkshire, *Twatt* in Orkney, *Fanny Barks* in Durham, *Brown Willy* in Cornwall, *Crotch Crescent* in Oxford and *Minge* Lane which is also in Worcestershire.

And for the past few months there's my wife thinking I've been spending my time writing a *serious* book!

Another way I came up with of giving it away, that similar to posting it to people saves me handing it out in person, is to hide it in places where it'll be easily found. The amounts aren't always as big and sometimes the amount I hide just covers the cost of the item it's hidden in but I'm sure it's still a nice find for someone all the same.

One place I do it quite often is in bookshops like WH Smith's and Waterstones. I've read about people doing this kind of thing before and I thought it was a good idea so I started doing it myself. I don't pick any particular genre or author I just pick up any book and if it costs £9.99 I'll hide a tenner inside it. Or if it costs £17.99 I'll put £20 inside it. Sometimes I'll take notes with me that say 'have this book on me' or 'there's nothing like a good book - particularly when it's free!' and put it inside with the money. And although I don't pick specific books to hide it in, just for a bit of fun I'll sometimes hide it in books that are to do with making money such as 'How to get rich quick' or 'Easy ways to make money.' I'd love to be a fly on the wall and see the look on someone's face if they bought either of *those* two books and when they turned a page a twenty pound note fell out!

It'd be rather like the look on *your faces* when you turn to the index page at the back of this book and you find the tenner that's been clipped to it.

Though no doubt someone has gone in Waterstones and picked a book up off the shelf titled 'Easy ways to make money' and just flicked through the pages, seen the twenty pound note inside, took it out and put it in their pocket and then put the book back on the shelve and walked out again. And if you have, fair play to you - that's an *even easier* way of making money!

It's not only in big bookshops like Waterstones and WH Smiths where I'll hide money inside books. I also do it in second hand bookshops too. So someone somewhere will have gone in a second hand book shop, picked up a book that's got a tenner hidden inside it and paid fifty pence for it not realising they're getting £9.50 change!

It'd be a bit like the bloke at the petrol station that when he went in to pay for his petrol he was told that it'd already been paid for and was then given £20 'change' by the cashier. Or £19.99 change if he's an idiot like me who can never stop the digit counter dead on thirty quid.

And as well as hiding money inside books I also hide it inside clothes. Oh, but before we leave the subject of finding money in books. How many of you have just turned to the index page to see if there *really was* a tenner there? You did didn't you! Well no wonder you couldn't find it. I didn't even include an index page in the book let alone a tenner clipped to it!

When I hide it inside clothes I'll go in places like Primark or Matalan and take a few pairs of jeans into the changing rooms as though I'm trying them on and if the jeans cost £29 I'll put £30 in one of the front pockets. Chances are the money won't be found until someone buys a pair because for some reason blokes don't usually put their hands in the pockets of jeans when they're trying them on. Well I don't anyway. I just have a look in the mirror to see if they're long enough, and if they look okay and they fit on the waist I'll take them off and take them to the counter and pay for them, as will most blokes. So it won't be until the guy that's bought them puts them on to wear one day and puts his hand in the pocket that he'll find the money. And I bet not many blokes take them back to the shop and say they've found thirty quid in the pocket that didn't belong to them!

But if I do the same thing with a pair of trousers I always put the money in the *back* pocket. That's because for some reason, unlike when buying a pair of jeans, us men *always* put our hands in the front pockets of trousers when we're trying them on. We then stand face on and look at ourselves in the full length mirror in the changing room. We'll then turn *side on* - with our hands still in the front pockets - and have a look at ourselves from the side. It's like we're on some kind of fashion parade! But at no point do we put our hands in the back pocket which is why I stick it in there as it's less likely to be found when someone's trying them on. And one reason we *don't* put our hand in the back pocket could be because we can never undo that little fidgety cotton loop that goes around the button. What a pain in the arse that can be at times when you're trying to get your wallet out. Although it's not quite as annoying as trying to undo the buttons on your flies when you're bursting to get *something else* out!

The inside pocket of a jacket is another good place to hide money as rarely does anyone put their hand in it when trying one on. You might look to see if it's *got* an inside pocket but you never put your hand in it do you? (I ask a lot of questions in this book don't I? And I've just done it again without even realising!) But now I've mentioned that no-one puts their hand into the inside pocket of a jacket, no doubt the next time you try a jacket on you *will* put your hand in there. And you'll probably now also put your hand in the back pocket of a pair of trousers and the front pocket of a pair of jeans! And when you do, hopefully I've been in the same shop the day before and left a few quid in each pocket for you.

One other place I hide it in clothes is in the pocket of an off the rail shirt. Most of these types of cotton shirts have a pocket on the top left or top right hand side with a little button on it and no one *ever* undoes it and puts their fingers in it when they're trying it on before they buy it. Thinking about it, I don't think I've ever put my fingers in the pocket of a shirt even after I've bought one, as don't probably nearly all blokes, and I've had some of my shirts for years. My wardrobe's full of them. So perhaps it's not such a good place to hide money after all as it may never get found! So if you happen to have bought an off the rail cotton shirt recently you may want to put this book down and nip upstairs and take a look in the pocket because you might find twenty quid in there.

Unfortunately for women it's only men that benefit when I give money away like this. And I'm not going to start sneaking women's clothes into the changing rooms with me just to even things up. I'd get some very funny looks indeed off the shop assistants if I was seen taking skirts and blouses in the men's changing rooms with me. And my wife might be slightly concerned too if word ever got back to her. And if you're thinking, 'Why does he shop in Primark and Matalan when he's worth £150 million?' Well as a rule, I don't, usually. Not that there's anything wrong with shopping in Primark or Matalan. And believe it or not my wife and kids sometimes shop there themselves, as have I on occasions. It's just that I'd rather - and I hope this doesn't sound demeaning - leave it in places like Matalan and Primark for the type of people who shop in there to find it as opposed to leaving it in shops on say Bond Street in Mayfair for the type of people who shop there for them to find.

When I say the 'type' of people that shop in Primark, I'm not suggesting for one minute that I think they're poor or common or that they may be in need of some kind of handouts. (Why do I get the horrible feeling that I'm digging a hole for myself here and sinking into it!) It's just that I think you'd agree that if someone bought a pair of jeans in Primark for £30 and then found £30 in the pocket, they'd be more appreciative of it than someone who bought a pair of jeans from a shop on Bond Street and *they* then found the equivalent of what they paid for them in the pocket, because money is probably of no object to most people who shop on places like Bond Street. Also, if I did it on Bond Street I'd have to leave at least *ten times* the amount in the pocket of a pair of jeans than I do in Matalan and Primark as it costs at least three hundred quid for a pair of jeans in Armani! (Can I climb back out of my hole now please?)

As I'm sure you're aware, a lot of people who shop in places like Armani and other expensive shops in London have got a lot of money. A *hell of a lot of money* in some cases and they are extremely wealthy. And most wealthy people don't go around boasting of their wealth or be flash about it. Yet some people can be. And although this next example of how I once gave money away came after I read something in the newspaper's a few years ago and then saw the video on YouTube, which gave me the idea to do a similar thing, I thought what this lot did and the way they did it was absolutely deplorable.

Chapter Nine There's A Right Way And There's A Wrong Way To Give Money Away

It isn't only in this country that I've given money away. I've given it away in other countries too. One place was Thailand, and one of the ways we did it (I was with two of my friends at the time) was to throw the money out of our hotel window.

I'd seen this done before during the 'yuppie era' in the 1980's when a group of city bankers who were making huge amounts of money on the stock exchange went on a trip abroad. I forget where they were exactly. Indonesia or Sri Lanka rings a bell. But wherever it was the locals were quite poor and what these bankers did was to stand on the roof of their hotel and throw money off it to the people below.

On the face of it you might think what they did was a nice gesture. But unlike the reasons me and my friends did it, which was for the benefit of the people we were throwing it to, *they* were doing it for their own gratification. And they could be heard laughing and commenting (as they swigged from £300 bottles of champagne) on the video they made what fun it was watching 'the poor little people' chase around for the money and fight each other for it. They also filmed themselves shaking the bottles of champagne and then spraying it on those below as they scrambled and fought for the money they were throwing off the roof. One of them also urinated off the roof onto the crowd as his friends laughed and egged him on.

By anybody's standards that's low. But the way we did it was completely different.

In contrast to how they did it (in the middle of the day, stood on the roof for all to see) and threw bundle after bundle of notes which turned out to be local currency with the approximate equivalent value of just ten pence per note, and which they used so that it would look on video as though they were giving away much more money than they actually were, and which caused mass hysteria, fights and scuffles and forced traffic to come to a standstill, *we* threw just one or two $50 bills at a time from our hotel window. And we did it very late at night/early in the morning at around 2am or 3am when we got in from a night out and when there were less people around. We also waited until only one or two people were passing and we'd just drop one fifty dollar bill each. That way they didn't start arguing and fighting with each other over it. Sometimes we'd make a paper plane out of it and throw it and watch as it floated down and landed in front of them, and when they picked it up you could see them looking up thinking 'where the hell's that come from!' It *really must* have seemed like pennies, or in this case Thai Baht, had fallen from heaven for those who didn't see us throw it! But sometimes we'd shout first so the person looked up and saw us and we'd say, "Here, catch," and drop it out of the window and when they caught it and saw how much it was they'd shout, "Thank You," and give us a big wave and a VERY big smile. And some would wave and say thank you and then give a little bow with their hands held together in front of them like they do when they're praying or visiting a temple. It was really quite humbling and you could just tell that they were extremely appreciative of it, probably even more appreciative than most of the people I've given money to in *this* country. Though like I said previously, I'm sure that everyone I've given money to here has appreciated it as well. But considering that fifty dollars is around the average weekly wage in Thailand you can understand just how happy they must have felt when as they were walking down the street the equivalent of their pay packet dropped into their hands.

We did this on most of the nights we were there and probably dropped in the region of four to five thousand dollars. And although we didn't cause as much chaos and pandemonium as the yuppie wanker's did, sorry, I mean yuppie *bankers* (or was I right first time?) we did notice slightly more people walking past our hotel at three o'clock in the morning (looking skywards) towards the end of our holiday than we did at the beginning of it!

As well as those walking past our hotel who benefited from our 'far eastern giveaway,' several others did too, including these two women I'm going to tell you about, though I did get a bit of a 'ticking off' afterwards for giving money to one of them. Well not so much a ticking off, it was more a bit of friendly advice not to do it as the circumstances weren't quite what they seemed.

The first woman I gave money to was sat outside the gent's toilet in this bar and she was handing out pieces of toilet paper as you go in in exchange for a few Baht. Nearly every bloke just walked straight past her and didn't give her anything. And most of those blokes didn't really need to 'buy' a few pieces of toilet paper anyway as they were only going for a pee and therefore only needed to use the urinal. But a few of those that walked straight past her were going for a 'dump,' or a crap as you may refer to it as. Or as one of my friends rather charmingly refers to it as, 'a clear out.'

Now one or two of those blokes who went for a clear out had the foresight to look and see if there was any toilet paper in the cubicle before they sat down, and on seeing that there wasn't any came back out again and begrudgingly bought a few sheets from the lady sat outside. However, one or two *didn't* have the foresight to look before they sat down. And if you happened to be in the toilets yourself using the urinal when they'd just finished clearing themselves out and they realised there wasn't any toilet paper, you'd hear shouts of, 'Fucking Hell!' and 'Oh Bollocks,' and 'Shit!' And considering the circumstances, the last of those three was probably the most appropriate to shout! These shouts were then usually followed by,

"Here mate, you couldn't do us a favour could you and get me some bog roll off her outside!" And if you were the cruel type with a wicked sense of humour (like me) you'd reply, "Certainly, no problem," and then leave and walk straight past the woman and go back to your table and tell your mates what happened and have a good laugh about it. And ten minutes later you'd all be laughing again as the bloke comes out of the toilet with a stern look on his face and walking rather awkwardly!

Anyway, so when I went to the toilet this lady handed me a few pieces of toilet paper so I took them even though I didn't need them. I then put my hand in my pocket and took out a couple of notes and gave them to her and she nearly fainted and fell off her chair. Because what I gave her, two one thousand Thai Baht notes, which at the time was around £55 in English money, was probably the equivalent of what she'd have got in six months sat outside that toilet trying to sell pieces of tissue.

We found out later that the bar owners used to 'auction' the chairs outside the toilets that the women sat on to the locals and the highest bidder could sit there for that week selling toilet paper. They also deliberately didn't put any toilet paper in the cubicles and instead gave it to the auction winner to sell.

It's quite an entrepreneurial idea actually, though somehow I can't see Wetherspoons taking it on! Having said that, didn't Michael O'Leary, the CEO of Ryanair once say that he was considering doing something similar by charging passengers to use the toilet during flights? Or was that just another one of his wind ups like the one where he said he was going to introduce standing areas on his planes so he could squeeze more passengers on board in order to make more money? (Though I do believe it's true that none of his office staff are allowed to charge their mobile phones at work because they'd be using the electricity that he pays for.)

And similar to the lady that spent all night sat outside the gents lavatory earning a living, the other woman I gave money to also spent the night sat down earning a living. However at the time I had no idea she was 'working' when I saw her sat on the kerb by the edge of the road holding a tiny baby.

She was sat by a busy main road where all the bars and restaurants where and we were on the opposite side about to cross over, and as we crossed I noticed her sat on the kerb opposite. She was sat upright but she had her eyes closed and she looked like she was fast asleep and as we got closer I could see she was holding something in her arms. But it wasn't until I got up close to her that I saw it was a newborn baby. And if it wasn't newborn then it couldn't have been no more than six months old.

It was night time too. Well actually it was early morning, it was about 2.am. And I said to my friends, "How bad is that?" and one of them replied, "Yes, it's very sad." And it *was* sad, but not quite as sad as I imagined. So I tapped her on her shoulder and when she opened her eyes I gave her 3500 Baht. She must have still been half asleep because she didn't realise I'd just given her nearly half the average monthly wage that someone earns in Thailand. (The average wage is between 5000 to 8000 Baht, £150 - £200 a month.) And it wasn't until we were around twenty yards away that she realised what I'd given her and she was ecstatic, and she stood up and started saying what I presume were very kind words and thanking me in Thai. So I gave her a wave and a smile and turned to go into this bar and as we did this huge Thai security guard/doorman who was sat outside said,

"Oi, you. Come here," and pointed at me and stood up. He didn't say it in a particularly aggressive manner but the fact that he would've dwarfed Arnold Schwarzenegger if he'd have stood next to him and he had half an ear missing and he looked like he'd be capable of giving Mike Tyson a run for his money, made us slightly nervous as we walked over to him! But we needn't had been nervous because despite his appearance he was very polite and he said, "I saw what you did then and it was very kind of you. But don't be fooled." And when I asked him what he meant he explained that the baby wasn't hers and that the real mum would have 'rented it out' to the woman for the night. And that the next night the baby would be in the arms of a different woman who would also be sat by a road somewhere, or the same woman would be sat in the same place with a different baby.

I was gobsmacked at first and thought what kind of a mother would rent their own baby out? But after thinking about it, if you're living in poverty, like a lot of people in Thailand are, and you're desperate and you have very little money to buy food for your baby in the first place you might have no alternative but to do something like that.

Apparently it's a very common thing for new mums to do. And it's sad enough to think that some people have to go to the lengths of sitting by the roadside all night holding a baby in the hope they'll be given money by unsuspecting tourists, but it's even sadder that some mums have to rent their children out to make ends meet.

It beggars belief and any parent reading this probably can't quite get their head around the idea of letting someone borrow their newly born baby for the night to go begging with. And seeing and hearing about such things makes you realise just how lucky - people like myself in particular - we are, and never to take anything for granted. And it's stories like these that I relay to my kids to remind them how EXTREMELY lucky *they* are and NEVER to take anything for granted. But like I've already said about them, they never do, and I'm sure they never will.

Back in England there were two other women I helped out who had kids with them and although they were no-where near as desperate as the woman who was sat by the side of the road in Thailand I still wanted to help. Though it wasn't so much helping them out financially it was more a case of coming to their rescue. Having said that I did still fork out nearly seven grand to rescue them!

I was at the airport one day checking in for a flight to Dubai and there was a lady with her young son who was checking in for a flight to Canada at the desk next to me and she was in tears because she'd just been informed by the girl who was checking people in that there had been a 'mix up' with her booking and her flight was full and there were no seats left for her and her son. Although it transpired that there hadn't been a mix up at all. The airline had just overbooked the flight like they always do but unfortunately for the airline - and for this lady and her son - everyone who had booked on the flight turned up.

You may not be aware of this but it's common practice for airlines to overbook flights. They don't overbook by many, only by around eight to ten seats. But they take the gamble that not everyone will turn up for their flight and most of the time it pays off because believe it or not, not everyone who books and pays for their flight turns up for it. The only problem for the airline is that when everybody who is booked on the flight turns up there aren't enough seats. They are then confronted with frustrated and angry passengers, or in the case of this woman, a very upset one.

I really can't understand why airlines are allowed to get away with overbooking flights. It's wrong. I can see why they do it, because they make more money. If a seat costs three hundred pounds and they overbook a flight by ten people then that's an extra three thousand pounds they've made on that flight. And if they do it on *every* flight *every* day of the week then they're making hundreds of thousands of pounds extra. So it's worth them taking the gamble even if say that in only one in twenty of the flights everyone who's booked on it turns up. But it still shouldn't be allowed. If a house builder like Barrett or Bovis where to buy a plot of land to build three hundred houses on and advertised that they were building three hundred and ten and sold off plan and took three hundred and ten deposits off people knowing that they were only going to build three hundred, they'd get sued. They just wouldn't be allowed to do it - not that they *would* do it. So why are airlines allowed to get away with doing it?

Anyway, as I was checking my luggage in I could hear what was being said to the woman by the girl on the check in desk and I heard what this woman was saying back. And the gist of the conversation was that the woman was saying that she and her son had to get on the flight as they were going to see her parents who lived in Vancouver. But she was being told by the girl on the check in desk that all the seats had gone and that all they could do was put her and her son on the next available flight but which wasn't until the following day, which as well as the woman being extremely annoyed about she was also extremely upset.

The girl on the checkout said that she'd get someone from customer services to come and speak with her and asked the woman would she mind stepping aside so she could check other passengers in, which the woman did. Personally I wouldn't have budged and I'd have stayed put and insisted on being put on the flight.

So after I'd checked in I went over to the woman and said that I'd heard what was going on and how I thought it was disgraceful how airlines can get away with it. She was really upset and told me that she was only going for a week and that as a result of not being allowed on the flight she was now going to miss the first two days. And she was saying just how much her mum and dad were looking forward to seeing their grandson and she started to get *even more* upset. So I told her to wait where she was for ten minutes and that if the customer services representative came not to agree to anything, such as being transferred to another flight. I then went to find out if there were any other flights leaving for Vancouver that day and as luck would have it there was one a few hours later. So I went to the airline desk and asked if there were any seats available on the flight and the lady I spoke with said that there was. So I asked her how much they were and she said that they were £860, each. She also said that seats in business class were available at £2,800 each. So I went back to the woman and her son and told her that an alternative flight was available later that day at six o'clock. I then said to her, "You're probably going to find this very hard to believe and I haven't got time to explain, but if you want to get on it I'll pay for you and your son." She said, "*You'll* pay?"

I said, "Yes, I'll pay. It's not a problem, but like I say, I haven't got time to explain as I've got *my own* flight to catch." Not that I would have explained about me giving money away anyway even if I *did* have the time. But I really was in a bit of a rush to catch my own flight. So I went back to the airline desk with her and booked two tickets to Vancouver for her and her son. And much like *I* was gobsmacked when that security guard in Thailand told me that some mums rent out their newborn babies, this woman was equally gobsmacked. And then she was *doubly* gobsmacked when I paid for two business class tickets!

After she was handed her tickets by the lady on the desk (who also looked slightly gobsmacked that I'd bought them for someone I'd only met ten minutes earlier) I told her to go back to the customer services representative at the other airline and tell them that she wanted a full refund, which the airline would have been obliged to give her, plus ask for some form of compensation. I again said that I really didn't have the time to explain why I'd done it, so she thanked me, several times over, and I wished her a pleasant flight and I made my way to board my flight to Dubai. And we took off with me having £5,600 less in my bank account than I did when I arrived at the airport!

The second woman I helped out was at Euston station, and who was on the same train as I was.

I was on my way back from Manchester and as I was stood by the door waiting to get off the train as it came into Euston there was a young mum waiting to get off too. She had four kids with her. The oldest was around ten years old and he had a younger brother and sister who were about three and four years old. There was also a baby in a pram that looked to be about six months old. And as well as her three kids and a baby she was also lugging two big suitcases and had a rucksack on her back! And the pram wasn't a small pushchair type either. It was the bigger type pram, the Silver Cross type that a baby lays down in.

When the train stopped I helped her off with her suitcases and the pram and I jokingly said to her that she quite literally had her hands full and that it must have been a journey and a half travelling down to London with three kids, a baby, a pram, two suitcases and a rucksack on her back. And she said that it had been an absolute nightmare and that she'd originally planned to drive but her car broke down the day before. And added that she was going to cancel the trip but because she didn't want to disappoint her kids by not taking them away she decided to make the journey by train instead. She then thanked me for helping her with her suitcases and as she got hold of the handles of them she said, "I'll be glad when I get to the Isle of White!" and she smiled and said, "C'mon kids," and off they went.

I stopped for a moment and looked at her in disbelief as she walked away. Usually it's the other way around. People normally stand and look at *me* in disbelief after they've been taken totally by surprise by something I've done for them or by what I've given to them. Now *I* was the one who had been taken totally by surprise and was left stood looking in disbelief as I watched this woman walk off up the platform pulling two heavy suitcases with three young kids by her side, with the ten year old pushing a Silver Cross pram with a baby in it, and with a rucksack on her back! I've got four kids myself so I know just how hard it can be travelling with kids. It's stressful enough trying to organise a day out in the car let alone travel by train to the Isle of White all the way from Manchester. And if you've got a couple of kids yourself you'll know exactly what I'm talking about. It's difficult enough with mum *and* dad never mind a mum on her own. Making that journey would be tiring enough doing it by yourself never mind doing it with suitcases, prams and kids and a rucksack on your back!

Just imagine how hard that journey would have been for her doing it the way she'd planned. Getting on and off trains and then up and down escalator's on the underground, getting on the tube, getting off the tube, up yet more escalators, getting another train to Portsmouth and then catching the ferry to the Isle of White. She'd have been worn out before her holiday had even started.

The only plus point about that journey was that she might have found two hundred quid inside the Metro newspaper on the underground that some odd ball had hidden in there!

When I got through the barrier at the end of the platform I saw her stood on the concourse so I went up to her and said, "Did you say you were travelling to the Isle of White?" and she said yes and that she was catching the ferry later that afternoon. I said, "Wait there. I'll be back in two minutes," and I went outside and asked a taxi driver how much it would cost to the ferry terminal at Portsmouth and he said it would cost approximately £120. I then went to the cash machine before going back in and telling the woman that if she wanted I'd pay for a taxi to take her to the ferry terminal in Portsmouth. I got the usual puzzled look and the 'why' questions but I just told her that I had four kids myself and I knew how hard it must be making a journey like that with them and that I wanted to help, and not surprisingly she gladly accepted the offer!

So I helped her with her cases to the taxi and after the driver had put her cases in the boot and just about squeezed the pram in after collapsing it, when she sat down in the back I gave her £1,000 that I'd just withdrawn from the cash dispenser. She looked flabbergasted and asked, "Is that how much it costs for a taxi from here to Portsmouth?" I said, "No. It only costs around a hundred and twenty but that'll also pay for a taxi to your hotel from the port in the Isle of White plus your return journey too. And you can use the rest to get your car fixed." And I shut the door and off she went to continue her journey under slightly less stressful circumstances.

Although for the first few hundred yards it may well have been slightly uncomfortable for her sat there like she was with her head twisted right around like she was re-enacting that scene from the film The Exorcist and staring at me out of the back window until I was out of sight wondering who the hell I was and not quite believing what had just happened to her!

The only slight hiccup with that one was that the taxi driver didn't have enough booster seats for the kids to sit on and he had to ask his mates in the cab rank if he could borrow a couple of theirs. And no doubt that young mum got a bit of a boost too knowing that she didn't have to traipse across London with her kids and luggage, getting on and off trains and up and down escalators and that on her return she'd be able to get her car fixed. And hopefully when she went to get her car repaired the garage where she took it wasn't as devious as the one I once took my wife's car to, to get hers repaired.

Chapter Ten Cheeky Sods And Ageing Mod's

Did you know that I once paid for fifty MOT's to be done? That's a bit of a silly question to ask really isn't it because obviously you *wouldn't* know that I'd once paid for fifty MOT's to be done because I've never told anyone before until now! But it was just a rhetorical question that linked nicely to this next story.

I didn't pay for fifty MOT's to be done on the same car by the way. It'd be a right old banger if it failed its MOT fifty times. Though a friend of mine does own a Rolls Royce that *looks* like it has failed its MOT fifty times. It's a Rolls Canardly - it can roll down hills but it can hardly get back up them! (Private joke that one.)

A warning light had been coming on in my wife's Range Rover so I took it to a garage near to where I live to get it looked at. I'd never used this particular garage before as I'd always taken it to the main Range Rover dealership but they'd recently moved and for what I thought it would be worth I thought I may as well take it somewhere nearer rather than drive the nearly forty miles to where the main dealer had moved to.

Now I'm not saying that all garages are like this

because I know they're not but when some garage's see an expensive car coming in, and if they think the owner is well off then they tend to hike their hourly labour rate from around £30 per hour to around £50 or £60. And remarkably, the repairs also seem to take several hours longer than they would if the garage *didn't* think you were well off. So instead of being billed *two hundred* and fifty pounds you end up getting billed *four hundred* and fifty pounds. And I got the feeling this was going to happen to me after I spoke to one of the mechanics. And I wasn't wrong either because they gave me a quote for £425! A bit of a cheeky sod? Well that's *one way* of describing him though I think *a right fucking cheeky bastard* is a much better way because even though I don't know a great deal about cars I thought their quote was *just a little* bit on the steep side. So I politely told them I'd let them know when I'd decided what I was going to do and left.

A week or so later I mentioned it to a friend of mine (the same one with the Rolls Canardly) who told me to take it to someone *he* knew who owned his own garage. So I did, and as soon as I started speaking to the owner I got a totally different feeling than I did when I spoke to the mechanic at the first garage.

I showed him the warning light that kept coming on and he got his diagnostic machine and tested it and he said that it'd be just a fuse or a loose connection and he'd sort it there and then. So he told one of the lads that worked there to make me a cup of tea and said for me to take a seat in the waiting area. And no sooner had I sat down and watched his mate fill the kettle with water he came back in and gave me the key and said it was all sorted. His mate didn't even have time to put the tea bag in the cup it was done that quickly! And when I asked him how much I owed him he said, "Nothing." Then when I said that I thought I really should pay him he said, "What for? I didn't use any parts and it only took me five minutes. Don't worry about it."

So that just shows what some people are like. This guy *knew* I had money and that I was very wealthy yet he didn't charge me a penny. But the guy at the other garage just *presumed* I had money (and presumed right) and wanted to charge me four hundred and twenty five quid. And as much as I insisted he took something he wouldn't. So when I next saw my friend who told me about the garage, I tried to give him some money for him to pass on to his friend who owned the garage but he too said not to worry about it. He then mentioned that his friend was in the process of opening an MOT test centre adjacent to his garage and it gave me an idea of a different way I could 'pay' him but it meant letting his friend in on the secret of me giving money away. My friend said it wouldn't be a problem if we told him because he could be trusted not to say a word to anyone. So we went to see his pal at the garage and I told him what I'd been doing and said that I had an idea that would benefit both of us - in more than one way. It would benefit us in *four ways* to be exact.

I asked him how much he was going to be charging for an MOT when he opened the test centre and he said it'd be £50. So I told him that I'd give him £2,500 to cover the cost of fifty MOT's and I'll also pay for an advert in the local paper saying that as an opening promotion the first fifty are free. That way, one, I'd still be kind of 'giving' money away to people like I'd already been doing. Two, it would be a good way of getting publicity for the test centre plus fifty people would be getting a free MOT. Three, it would be a way of me thanking him for sorting out the problem on my wife's car and not charging me. And four, hopefully it'd take a bit of business off the cheeky bastard at the garage down the road that tried to rip me off for four hundred and twenty five quid!

So that's what we did. And if you were one of those fifty people who got a free MOT hopefully your car passed first time and it didn't fail. (Unlike my friend's clapped out Rolls 'Canardly' that *always* fails its MOT!)

As you know, the point of me giving money away is to brighten up someone's day, and brighten up someone's day it certainly did whilst down on the south coast one weekend. Though considering where we were you could say it *Brighton'd* up this person's day.

One of the five friends who I gave £100k too is an aging 'Mod' as in the 'Mod's and Rockers' era of the mid sixties to early seventies. And like the many thousands of MOD's that are still around today he still has a scooter and is a member of a scooter club, and throughout the year they go on scooter rallies all over the country. One of those rally's takes place in Brighton over the August bank holiday weekend and as a kind of thank you for me giving him the money he paid for us all to go to it and stay for a few days.

I've never been to a scooter rally before and I couldn't believe just how many people turned up. There were hundreds, if not thousands of them on scooters. They were everywhere. It was like a scene from the film Quadrophenia! Some of them were *even dressed* like the cast from Quadrophenia, including my friend who sported a knee length parker with the red, white and blue target on the back. (One night he donned a Union Jack jacket like the one guitarist Pete Townsend from the band 'The Who' - who were my friend's and most other MOD's favourite band during the MOD era - used to wear on stage. And in which my friend looked absolutely ridiculous and got ~~a bit~~ a lot, of stick for!)

The other thing I couldn't believe, or didn't realise, was just how many homeless people there are in Brighton. They too, like those on scooters were everywhere (and one or two of them looked smarter than my friend did in his Union Jack jacket!) And I do mean everywhere. And anyone who has visited Brighton recently or who lives there will know exactly just how bad the problem of rough sleepers and homeless people is in the area. It's on a par with London. We walked past one hotel on the seafront, the Jury's Inn, and there were two single mattresses right outside the entrance with bags and belongings on one and someone fast asleep on the other. People were stepping over the fella that was asleep on it to get into the hotel. And someone had also pitched a tent a little further along the pavement and were living in that. I've never seen anything like it.

We weren't staying in this hotel, we were staying in the Premier Inn around the corner, "The Premier Inn?" You all gasp! "He's got all that money and he stays in a Premier Inn!"

Well, firstly, just like I sometimes shop in Matalan and Primark, I sometimes stay in budget hotels. Secondly, according to my friend who treated us to the weekend away, the Hilton up the road was fully booked (or so he says.) And thirdly, I quite like the Premier Inn and their beds are some of the most comfiest I've slept in. In fact, I've stayed in hotels that cost over a £1,000 a night and the beds are nowhere near as comfortable as the 'Hypnos' beds you get in a Premier Inn.

The pro's and con's of the Premier Inn in Brighton is that on the plus side its location is ideal because it's right in the city centre. The only downside is that there is no onsite parking and you have to use the NCP car park at the back of the hotel which costs £30 for 24 hours, and that's WITH a hotel discount! And as wealthy as I am, one bugbear I have is being fleeced in car parks, particularly NCP one's which are extortionate. And it infuriates me even more that in some car parks you have to put your registration number in when buying a ticket which then appears on the ticket itself. The aim of which is to prevent people from giving their ticket to other people on the way out to save them having to pay.

Ironic really isn't it that I don't mind giving people who I've never met before £100 in a car park for no reason whatsoever but it irritates me having to pay seventy quid less to park my own car in one!

The hotel was above a row of shops, one of which was empty and the doorway was being used by a homeless guy who we saw every morning and every evening as we walked past. And when we walked past in the morning he'd always say 'hello' and 'have a nice day' and on our way back at night he'd always ask if we'd had a nice evening. But not once did he ask us for any money. Now any cynics reading are probably thinking that he was only being polite hoping that in return we'd give him some change, and that may well be the case. But the fact that he *didn't* ask for anything actually made me want to give him something. So if you cynics are right and that *was* his ploy then it worked!

The only problem with giving money to some of the people you see sleeping rough on the streets is that you don't know if they're going to spend it on drugs or alcohol. I dare say a lot of them do. But then again if it brightens up *their* day a little bit just like it brightens up someone's day when I give them £100 in a car park or leave it in a cash dispenser for them, does it really matter? I suppose the right answer is 'yes, it does matter' as you don't really want to fuel their addiction. But in the bigger scheme of things, giving an alcoholic or a drug addict a hundred quid isn't going to make a great deal of difference to them in the long term. But I wasn't intending to give this guy any money anyway. I was going to give him something a lot better: some clean clothes, a roof over his head and an exceptionally comfy bed to sleep on for a few nights, although I did end up giving him some money as well.

Now I probably wouldn't have got away with doing this in most hotels as normally the reception is on the ground floor and usually you have to walk past the reception desk to get to the lifts to get to the floor your room is on. But because of the layout of the hotel, the reception at the Premier Inn in Brighton is on the first floor and you only really need to go there when checking in or out. Otherwise you can just get in the lift on the ground floor and go straight up to the floor your room is on, which made it ideal for what I was planning on doing.

We had two rooms and we were due to check out of them on the Tuesday. So on the bank holiday Monday I asked the receptionist if the room that me and one of my friends was in was available for a few more days and she said that it was and that it was available until the following Sunday. So I told her that I wanted to keep that room on and paid for the following five nights. I then went down to a menswear shop in the town centre, and having seen the guy in the doorway for the past few days I had a rough idea of his height and build so I bought a couple of pairs of jeans (I checked the front pockets but no-one had left thirty quid in them!) a few T shirts, a jumper and some socks and underwear. The only thing I couldn't gauge by looking at him was his shoe size. So I took a gamble and bought a pair of trainers in a size nine and put the receipt inside the box so he could take them back and exchange them if they didn't fit.

On our way out on the Monday night he was there again and as we walked past, as usual, he said that he hoped we had a nice night. We said thanks and I asked him if he'd be here in the morning at around ten o'clock and he said that he would be. Then on our way back later that night as we walked past him I said, "See you in the morning," and I gave him a cup of coffee and a sandwich I bought for him from 'Subway' opposite. He was really made up, and with a big smile said, "Oh thanks mate!" I thought to myself, 'I've got a funny feeling you'll be *far more* made up and have an *even bigger* smile on your face in the morning.' And we left him drinking his coffee and eating his sandwich which hopefully made him feel a little better as he went to sleep that night than he did most other nights. Though I dare say he probably didn't sleep much wondering why I'd asked him if he'd be there the following morning.

The next day my two friends checked out of the other room and as we all left the hotel I said to them that I'd meet them outside the NCP car park once they'd collected the car.

I told them I'd meet them *outside* the car park for two reasons. A, because as they already knew, I was going to go and see the guy who'd been sleeping rough in the doorway to give him his surprise. And B, so *one of them* would have to pay the £30 parking fee and not me!

I then walked over to the guy in the doorway and told him to get his stuff, which comprised of a hold all and a couple of shopping bags, and to come with me as I had a surprise for him. So he got up and followed me and as we went through the hotel doors he stopped and said, "I can't go in there." So I told him that he could and not to worry and that it'd be fine. We then got in the lift and went up to the fifth floor and went in the room and I said to him, "This is yours until Sunday."

"Mine?" he replied with a *very* peculiar look.

"Yes," I told him. "Yours. And these are yours too," and pointed to the clothes and trainers I'd bought for him that I'd laid out on the bed. And then I said, "And that money's yours too," and pointed to ten twenty pound notes that were lying on the table. I'd even ran a bath for him and left a clean towel out!

If the phrase 'you could have knocked me over with a feather' ever applied, it applied here. He was bewildered. Totally lost for words.

I told him the room was his until the following Sunday and that it was still in my name (really it was in my friend's name but he wasn't to know that) and that I trusted him not to bring anyone else back and more importantly not to take anything when he left that didn't belong to him. And he assured me that he wouldn't. Though I must admit I did feel like taking the bed home myself because it was that comfy! And he must have been true to his word because my friend who booked it never heard anything back from the hotel.

'A good night's sleep guaranteed?' as the Premier Inn's motto goes. I bet they were the best five nights sleep that bloke had had in months. And he got some clean clothes and a couple of hundred quid to boot.

My friend who booked the hotel told me later that it wouldn't have really mattered if that guy had stolen anything from the room or caused any damage as he hadn't booked it in his real name. Because for a bit of a laugh and because it was the MOD weekend he'd booked it under the name of one of Pete Townsends fellow band mates from The Who, their wild man drummer Keith Moon, who was my friend's idol when he was younger. Keith Moon also had a reputation for hurling television sets out of hotel windows. Fortunately for that homeless guy who had been sleeping rough in the shop doorway below, televisions in hotel rooms are fixed to the wall these days. Otherwise, if my friend had returned to his room one evening and decided to imitate his idol, that guy may well have woken up one morning with a very sore head!

That and the 'Miss X' one are probably the most satisfying giveaways I've done. I can't begin to imagine just how much that would have meant to that bloke. Probably the only people that would realise just how much something like that would mean to someone who sleeps rough would be those who sleep rough themselves. Picture sleeping in a shop doorway next to a hotel or on a mattress on the pavement *outside* a hotel in the rain and cold and you'd not had a change of clothes or a shower for months on end, and then all of a sudden you were given a room *in* that hotel along with some new clothes and £200 and a pair of £75 trainers (that quite possibly were the wrong size!) It might not seem a great deal to the ordinary person on the street but to someone who *sleeps rough* on the streets you can guarantee it certainly *would* mean a great deal to them. And that guy probably felt like his numbers had come up on the lottery - without even playing it.

And that's what life is I suppose, a bit of a lottery. Some people are lucky in life and others, like that homeless guy, *aren't* so lucky. And as well as each and every one of us playing our own part in the lottery of life, most of us play the actual lottery itself. And even though I myself may well fall into the bracket of one of life's lucky ones, without fail I still play the lottery every Wednesday and Saturday.

Chapter Eleven Life Is Just A Lottery

I play the lottery every week despite the fact that if I won the jackpot it'd make very little difference to my lifestyle. It wouldn't make any difference at all to my lifestyle to be honest, even if I won a rollover of £20 million because I'll never get around to spending the millions I've already got let alone another £20,000,000 on top!

People think it's odd when I tell them I play the lottery because I'm a multi millionaire as it is and I was already a millionaire when I first started playing it. But I've played it since day one and like a lot of people I have the same numbers that I put on every week and I feel like I dare not stop playing it just in case my numbers come up, even though I wouldn't need the money if I won. And with the odds of winning the jackpot being around fourteen million to one my numbers probably *never will* come up. But I still play it every Saturday and Wednesday and that's the problem with having the same numbers. They're in your head and you know what they are and it's the fear of not putting them on and them coming up that forces us to continuing playing. That's why there was such an outcry when Camelot, who run the

National Lottery, introduced the Wednesday draw with the same numbers, 1 - 49, as it was then. They could have quite easily used numbers 50 - 99 but they knew that if they did that not as many people would play. So they kept numbers at 1 - 49 knowing that most people used the same fixed numbers every Saturday and in the back of people's minds (millionaires like myself included) they'd think that they'd better play on Wednesday as well using the same numbers just in case they came up. In hindsight, probably like everybody else, I wish I'd have just had a lucky dip in the very first draw instead of choosing my numbers based on birthdays, my kids ages, my house number (which I'm not telling you!) and how many legs my dog had. "One of his Lotto numbers is four," you all shout! Well you're all wrong. One of my numbers is two and that's because my dog only had two legs! Seriously, it did. It lost both its hind legs after it was run over by a car and we had those wheels fitted to it that you can now get for dogs. And it had like a trolley type thing attached to the back of it as well with a cover on it. People used to mistake him for a mini rickshaw driver when we took him out! But the advantage of having a lucky dip as opposed to having *fixed* numbers based on birthdays and your house number and what not that get stuck in your head and that you'll always remember, is that you *don't* remember the numbers of lucky dips because they're different ones every week. Therefore, if whilst out shopping one Saturday afternoon you forgot to do the lottery you wouldn't be that bothered when you got home and realised you hadn't put it on - and you wouldn't find yourself legging it up the street to your local Co-op at ten past seven that same Saturday night in the pouring rain like you would if you forgot to put your usual fixed numbers on! And the fact that the odds of winning the jackpot are fourteen million to one won't deter people from *not* sprinting up the high street at ten past seven on a Saturday night to put their usual numbers on if they've forgotten to do so even if it *is* pissing down. Because you'll be sat there thinking to yourself 'I best had go and put the lottery on because it'll be just my luck I don't do it and my numbers will come up.' Which when you think about it is quite stupid. And it's stupid for two reasons. Firstly, if at ten past two on a Saturday afternoon someone said to you that a horse was running in the 2.30 at Ascot and it was fourteen million to one, you wouldn't run to the bookies to put a fiver on it would you? Because you know that if the bookies are offering odds of fourteen million to one then it's got absolutely no chance of winning. My two legged dog – pulling it's rickshaw with me sat on it – would have more chance of winning! And the second reason it's stupid is because you can now play the Lotto online. So you can put your usual numbers on from the comfort of your armchair using your phone without getting piss wet through running to the Co-op! But it just shows how much of a hold it has over you even though it's now *even harder* to win the jackpot since they added more numbers a couple of years ago.

I'm sure I'm not the only millionaire that plays the lottery, though whether other millionaires would give it all away if they won the jackpot like I would is another thing. But have you ever wondered what you'd do if you *did* win the lottery? I'm sure you have as it's everyone's dream. Endless holidays, a big house, nice cars and so on. But how do you think you'd react if you were sat there one Saturday night and your numbers came out of 'Merlin' and you were suddenly catapulted into a rich and famous lifestyle. (Why do they bother giving the machines names, and stupid one's at that, like Guinevere, Lancelot and Galahad? Who cares?)

I think most people would find it hard to

contain themselves and they'd jump that high that their heads would go through the ceiling. They'd then probably swing naked from the lampshade before picking up the phone and ringing all their family and friends to tell them the good news. Although considering that nearly everybody has got a smart phone these days they'd more than likely just 'face time' them instead. And if they *did* face time their friends and family hopefully they'd remember to put their clothes back on beforehand after swinging naked from the lampshade!

You'd be elated, and naturally so and it'd be a perfectly natural instinct for most people to want to tell everyone. But then you'll also get those that say they wouldn't tell anybody, apart from may be their family, and try and keep it a secret. But it would be a very hard secret to try and keep. None more so than trying to keep it a secret from your neighbours.

If someone like myself won the lottery it would be very easy for me to keep it a secret as my lifestyle wouldn't change. My neighbours don't see me leaving to go to work every morning at 7.00am, I already live in a big house, I own expensive cars and I regularly go abroad on luxury holidays and cruises as well as owning my own yacht (I'll come to that shortly.) But if you didn't already have that lifestyle it would be extremely difficult for you to keep your lottery win a secret. It wouldn't be long before the neighbours noticed you'd stopped going to work at seven o'clock in the morning - and then stopped going to work altogether. And they might think it a bit odd if you suddenly put your house up for sale and went on a world cruise. And the net curtains would start to twitch up and down the street if you pulled up outside your house in a brand new Ferrari one day. And if you were towing a luxury 80ft yacht on the back of your Ferrari when you pulled up then your neighbours may well twig that Guinevere had spat your numbers out the Saturday before. Though having said that you wouldn't be able to tow your new yacht on the back of your Ferrari would you. Because as I explained when I was telling you about my caravan, Ferrari's don't have tow bars! Well mine hasn't anyway.

However some people *are* capable of keeping their win a secret. Even from those closest to them. Or those you *might think* were closest to them.

I once watched a programme about lottery winners and they had the person from Camelot on who went around to winner's houses to give them the cheque. And he said that when he went into this bloke's house who'd won the jackpot to sort the payment out, the bloke asked him how long it would take. So the guy from Camelot said it would only take around fifteen minutes or so and asked why, thinking he might be in a rush to go somewhere. And he said that he was a little bit shocked when the bloke replied, "No, I'm not in a rush to go anywhere. It's just that my wife is due back from work in half an hour and I haven't told her I've won and I'm not going to either."

Not only hadn't he told his wife he'd won the lottery, he let her carry on working too!

That story reminds me of a joke I once heard where a bloke runs into his house and shouts upstairs to his wife, "Pack a couple of suitcases I've just won the lottery!"
His wife shouts down, "Shall I pack for warm weather or cold?"
And her husband shouts back, "I couldn't give a fuck what you pack just get out."

But whether you kept it a secret or not, coming into that kind of money would take some adapting too. Trust me, it really would.

You read of stories of how some winners say it completely ruined their lives and how they wished they'd never won it. And the reason those winners say it ruined their lives is because they don't know how to handle money, or such a huge amount of money anyway. And they probably didn't realise the effect it can have becoming an instant millionaire. That's because there's a big difference between becoming a millionaire from winning the lottery and from becoming a millionaire by working for it or being born into it. I'm not suggesting that people who say it ruined their lives are stupid but if one day you're working nine to five and taking home £300 a week and the next week you've got £7 million in the bank, the impact must be immense. Your head would be spinning. That's why Camelot have advisors who provide 'after care' for lottery winners and they give them advice on how to handle their win. Some take the advice, some don't and say, 'sod the advice, just give me the cheque!' Which is fine if you think you can handle it. But my advice to anyone who won the lottery would be to listen to what the Camelot advisors say because it'll be worth it in the long run and it could quite possibly save your life from becoming a misery, because the advisors will 'teach' you how to handle becoming a millionaire and how to go on and live and enjoy the life of luxury you've always dreamed of.

The point I'm trying to make about there being

a difference between becoming wealthy by winning the lottery and becoming wealthy by earning it or inheriting it, is that in the latter, coming by such a huge amount of money hasn't happened overnight and you've become accustomed to having it over a period of time, and so you know how to handle it.

Take my kids for example. And there are occasions when I wish somebody *would* take them because they're a right pain in the arse at times! Particularly during the school holidays when they get bored, which I'm sure is a scenario familiar with most mums that are reading this book. But when they inherit *my* fortune (if I haven't given it all away by then!) it won't be a shock to them having twenty or twenty five million each in the bank which will enable them to live a luxury lifestyle because they'll already be used to living it having been brought up as such. Whereas coming into millions by winning the lottery literally does happen overnight. On the Saturday morning when you put the lottery on you could be down to your last twenty quid until pay day. And then on the Sunday morning when you check your ticket you've found you've won four or five million. So within the space of 24 hours you've gone from one end of the financial ladder to the other. However even though it may take you to the top of the *financial* ladder it doesn't necessarily take you to the top of the *social* ladder as some lottery winners seem to think it does.

Winning the lottery doesn't change the type of person you are. If you're working class and you win £5 million on the lottery and you move to a house in an upper class area it doesn't make you an upper class person. There's nothing wrong with moving to an upper class area, or a 'better' area, but you'll still be working class. I'm not being snooty here by the way and please don't think for one minute I'm having a pop at the working classes and being insultive towards them because I'm not. It's just that some people who suddenly come into large amounts of money try and pretend they're something they're not and they forget their background and where they've come from. Which probably *is* insultive to those they once lived amongst and to the friends and work colleagues - and in some cases possibly family members too - who they no longer bother with, and who no doubt *would* consider it an insult. One such person was on that same television programme I watched about lottery winners.

This bloke had won around £17 million on the rollover jackpot and he bought a big house in a very posh area. He joined the local golf club (I knew it well as I used to be a member of it before we moved house) and he joined a local tennis club too, even though he'd never played tennis in his life. And he started eating in very expensive restaurants and frequenting exclusive bars and clubs just so he could try to mingle and socialise with the local wealthy residents but he said that nobody wanted to know him. And the reason why nobody would've wanted to know him was because they would have been able tell just by listening to him that he was trying to be something he wasn't. He just wasn't 'one of their sort.' The upper classes and the wealthy don't go around bragging about how much money they've got like he was doing, they don't need too. And they conduct themselves in a way totally different from the way *he* was conducting *himself*. It would have been completely alien to him and he'd have stood out like a sore thumb. Listening to him reminded me of that scene in Only Fools and Horses when Del Boy was trying to fit in with the 'Yuppie crowd' and made a fool of himself when he fell through the bar hatch when he was stood next to Trigger. And I could well imagine this guy making a fool of himself too in front of those *he* was trying to fit in with by pretending to be the lord of the manor.

But in any walk of life, be it upper class, working class or middle class, the worst thing you can do is to pretend to be something you're not and try to put on a front because more often than not people will see right through you. And the type of people that bloke was trying to impress and get in with and become one of would have seen right through him like an X ray. As my dad used to say to me (as he was repairing my school shoes for the umpteenth time) and as I now tell my kids, "Just be yourself and you'll find that most people will warm to you."

Chapter Twelve From Jet2 To Jet Set

I'm not upper class myself. I'm middle class. But I also have many working class friends, and one of the nicest people I've ever met was from a working class background too, though unfortunately he'd just been made redundant so he wasn't actually working.

I met him in Majorca and as well as him being one of the nicest people I've ever met he was also one of the very few people I've ever given a cheque to as opposed to giving cash like I normally do. (The reason I don't often give cheques out is because they have your name and bank account details on them which could quite easily lead to my identity being revealed.)

We were on our yacht and we'd sailed from Marseille in the south of France to Majorca and we were moored at the marina in Puerto Portals which is situated in the bay of Palma next to neighbouring Portals Nous.

Puerto Portals is one of the most glamorous places in Majorca and is often compared to Puerto Banus in Marbella, and like Puerto Banus does, it attracts celebrities and the rich and famous. It's been reported that the likes of Paris Hilton, Brad Pitt, Jim Carrey and Jenson Button have been seen there as has Bill Gates and the King of Spain, though I haven't seen any of them there myself whenever I've been there. Although from a distance I did once think I'd seen Luciano Pavarotti all suited and booted on a makeshift stage by the quayside about to burst into song. But I soon realised it *wasn't* him when the music began to play and instead of him singing the opening lines to Nessun dorma he started belting out the 'Go Compare' song and it dawned on me that 'Pavarotti' was actually Wynne Evans filming a new advert! Though Wynne has got a very good voice I must admit.

Puerto Portals really is a beautiful place and with it being only around ten or fifteen minutes by car or bus from the popular holiday resorts of Palma Nova and Magaluf, as well as attracting the rich and the famous it also attracts lots of tourists including families who stroll around the marina sightseeing and looking at the yachts. And one family walked past one morning as I was getting the boat ready for a trip around the island. They were an English family from Yorkshire, a man and his wife with a young son who was five years old and their daughter who was three. And as I stepped off the boat the dad asked if the yacht was mine and when I said that it was he said what a nice boat it was and asked if I'd sailed it from England. I told him I hadn't sailed it *directly* from England and that when I'd bought it I'd had it delivered from Poole in Dorset where it was built to the port in Marseille where more often than not it was moored. And from there I'd sailed it to Puerto Portals.

He was very chatty and he was telling me about a documentary he'd seen that was made at a yacht maker's in Poole and he found it really interesting. I vaguely remembered the programme he was talking about as I'd seen it myself. If I remember rightly it was filmed at the Sunseeker shipyard in Poole Quay and then at the London boat show and it was about a new luxury yacht they were building. He couldn't believe the lengths - and costs - some buyers go to customising their yachts and he mentioned one part of the documentary where a buyer from America spent something like £125,000 replacing the marble in the bathroom because he didn't like the colour of it. He was laughing and said that that bloke had spent more replacing the marble in his bathroom than *he'd* paid for his house! And tongue in cheek added that he'd much prefer to have a week's self catering holiday in Palma Nova with Jet2 like he was having than holiday onboard a luxury yacht, which I found rather amusing.

We chatted for quite a while and I took an instant liking to him and I asked him if he'd ever been on board a yacht and when he said he hadn't I asked him if he and his wife and two kids would like to come aboard and take a look around. His face lit up and he said, "Really?!" I told him it was no problem at all and took him on board and introduced him to my wife and kids and then showed him around.

He was amazed by it and when we were at the

helm he asked was it okay if he took a few photographs of himself 'at the wheel' to send to his mates back home for a bit of a laugh cracking on he'd bought his own yacht. I said of course it was and left him and his wife to take a few pictures on their phones. I then went downstairs to where my wife was and asked her what she thought about inviting them out with us for the day. She said that she thought the same as I did that they were a very nice family and said that she wouldn't mind at all. So I went back 'up top' and asked them were they in a rush or had they any plans for the day and when he said they hadn't I asked them if they'd like to spend the day with us and go on a trip around the island – and his face lit up again!

I wouldn't usually, and I hadn't before or haven't since, invite total strangers onto my yacht and spend the day with them. And even though like other things I've done it was fairly impulsive I instinctively knew that there'd be no problems. I certainly wouldn't have invited a drunken group of lads, or girls for that matter, who'd come up from Magaluf for the day onto my yacht! But I felt totally at ease having this bloke and his family on board.

They had a fantastic day, as did we, and by the end of it both my wife and I felt like we'd known them for about ten years even though we'd only known them for about ten hours.

During the course of the day whilst talking to them he was telling me that he'd recently been made redundant from his job and at one point they were thinking of cancelling their holiday because they couldn't really afford it. But they decided to go ahead with it as it might be their last one for a while as there wasn't a great deal of work in the area where they came from and his prospects of finding a job weren't good. So I asked him how much his holiday had cost and he said that altogether it had cost in the region of £2,500.

When we got back to Puerto Portals and got off the yacht they both thanked us and said they'd had a wonderful day and asked us if we'd like to go for something to eat with them and that they'd pay for it as a way of thanking us, and he pointed to a restaurant at the end of the marina. Now bearing in mind that earlier that day he'd told me he'd been made redundant and was thinking of cancelling their holiday because they were struggling to pay for it, I thought that was a really nice gesture. I also think that if we'd have accepted his offer he may have had a heart attack when he got the bill after the meal because the restaurant he'd pointed to was one of the most expensive in the marina! To give you an idea of how much it costs to eat there, the starters alone cost around 35 Euros. And I doubt very much we'd have got a table anyway because even with prices like that it's nearly always fully booked every night of the week. So I thanked him for his offer and said that we already had a restaurant booked, which we did, and that he could be *our* guests and that *I'd* pay.

He was a bit reluctant at first to accept and said that they'd feel a bit cheeky if they let me pay considering they'd spent the day on our yacht, but I insisted, and so they agreed. We then went for a meal during which I discreetly asked at the bar if they had a small envelope I could have and the barman said he did and gave me a small white one.

At the end of the evening when it was time for them to go we were stood outside the restaurant and they thanked us again for such a wonderful day and I shook hands with him. And as I shook his hand I gave him the little white envelope and told him not to open it until he got in the taxi and was on his way back to Palma Nova. He looked slightly mystified and asked what was inside it, so I said it was just a little memento of the day for him to keep. He said thanks once more and he and his wife and two kids got into their taxi, and no doubt about 100 yards down the road when he opened the envelope his face would have lit up for a third time that day. That's because the 'memento' I'd given him was a cheque for £5,000 and I'd put a note in with it saying 'half of this will cover a week's self catering with Jet2 in Palma Nova next year and the rest will help tide you over until you find another job. Alternatively, you can use it to replace the marble in your bathroom!'

That bloke being how he was is a very good example of just being yourself and how by doing so people will warm to you. And unlike the bloke who won the lottery who was trying to pretend he was some kind of upper class gent and started to hang around in upmarket bars and joined the local tennis club etc trying to impress, this guy did nothing of the sort. He didn't go out of his way to try and 'get in' with a rich person who owned a yacht, he was just his normal friendly self and *I* certainly warmed to *him*.

Someone else I warmed to was a 'betting runner' at a dog track we once went to. I love going to the dogs and having a bet on the greyhounds and whenever we go we make a night of it and have a meal in the restaurant. It's a good night out and as those of you that have been will know, that as well as having table service with a waitress or waiter bringing you your food and drinks, someone also comes along prior to each race and takes your bets for you.

On this particular night my wife and I went with four of our friends and like we usually do when we go we had a £10 bet on each race. You don't have to bet that much, some people just have a couple of quid on each race or a pound even. Although if you go down to the track side you'll sometimes see 'real' or professional gamblers betting several hundred pounds at a time on a race.

The runner who was taking our bets was a young girl who was about twenty years old and she was really pleasant and never stopped smiling all night. And neither did I because I kept on winning! Out of the twelve races I won nine times. Even the runner couldn't believe my luck and she said it was very rare for someone to win so many races. She had a really beaming smile and every time she took our bets she had a quick chat and had a bit of a laugh and a joke and then when she came back to see if we had any winners she'd laugh and say, "Not again!" She must have got fed up saying it by the end of the night because I was winning that often! She really was a very pleasant girl.

At the end of the night what I usually do is leave a £20 tip for the waitress and a £20 tip for the runner. But after the penultimate race I said to my wife and friends that if I won the last race I'd give my winnings to the runner because she was such a nice girl, and they said that they'd do the same thing if *they* won. So we all looked at the race card to choose which dog we were going to back and at the same time we all said the same thing,

"It's got to be trap five!" That's because trap five was called 'service with a smile.' So we all put a tenner each on it and it won at 5/1!

The night couldn't have ended any better and when the girl came back to our table to see if any of us had won she looked at me and said, "Let me guess. You've won again!"

I said, "Correct! And so have they," and we all held up our slips, and with a big smile on her face she said, "That's brilliant!" We then gave her our slips and she counted out £360, and as she went to hand it to us I said, "Keep it. It's yours." She said, "Mine?"

I said, "Yes, it's yours. We all decided that before the last race that as well as leaving you a tip, if any of us picked the winner we'd give you the winnings too. And when we saw what trap five was called we all thought of you," and I handed her the race card and when she looked at it an even bigger smile appeared on her face!

I don't know what the protocol is for 'runners' and waitresses at the dogs, whether they pool their tips or if they keep them individually. But hopefully each keeps their own and she got to keep all of the £360 because she certainly did give service with a smile.

When I bet it's just for a bit of fun but I can see how for some people gambling becomes *more* than just a bit of fun and they become addicted to it. And I could well imagine it being a very slippery slope if you get bitten by the betting bug, and if you lose control and it gets a grip of you it'd become a very difficult grip to loosen. I don't need to gamble and you'll probably find that most wealthy people don't gamble at all simply because they don't need the money. I don't need the money either but I do like the excitement of having a bet on the horses or going to the dogs. I have a bet most Saturday's and I really enjoy putting a bet on at the bookies in the morning and spending the afternoon watching the racing at home on the television. I don't put a huge amount on, maybe £50 or £60 in total and if I win, I win, and if I lose, I lose. But even though I've got millions in the bank and I may only get £70 back if one of the horses I've backed wins, I still get really excited watching the race. My wife will sometimes walk in the room as the horses are nearing the finishing line and she'll start laughing when she sees me sat on the edge of the sofa shouting, "Come On, Come On!" at the television and to-ing and fro-ing backwards and forwards as if I'm riding the horse myself! It's daft when I think about it because one day earlier that week I may have concluded a business deal that had netted me a quarter of a million pounds. But when the deal was done I didn't jump out of my chair and start shouting, 'Yes! Yes! Get in there you beauty!' and start running around the room like a lunatic. I wouldn't have felt any emotion at all because it was just a business deal. Yet in the final furlong of a race that I'm watching on the television and I think I may win forty quid, I act like I'm Frankie Dettori on a bucking bronco! And if it wins I *do* run around the room like a lunatic, waving my betting slip in the air. Then I'll lick it and slap it on my forehead! The kids think I'm nuts!

Strange isn't it how I get more of a kick out of winning a few quid on the horses on a Saturday afternoon than I do securing a lucrative business deal?

The only problem with having a bet on a Saturday is that where I live there aren't any betting shops in the immediate area and there isn't one in the nearest village either so I have to drive around twenty minutes or so to the nearest one. I could have an online account I suppose but I prefer going into an actual bookies on a high street as there's more of an atmosphere and I enjoy chatting with the people in there.

Now you've probably never noticed this but rarely do you see betting shops in upmarket areas. You may see the odd one here and there but on the whole they're few and far between and they're not that busy either. Yet in *not so* upmarket areas you'll see several on the same street. Quite often two or three of which are owned by the same company like William Hills or Corals. There was one street in Newham in East London that was in the news a few years ago that didn't just have *a few* betting shops on its high street, it had EIGHTEEN!

The reason you don't see many in 'posh' areas is because like I said, the majority of most wealthy people don't bet on the horses. But then again the majority of most *not so* wealthy people don't bet on the horses either. So why would a betting shop company want to open three shops on the same street? Well the answer isn't because they want to try and get more people to have a flutter on the gee-gees. The focus is on the FOTB's - Fixed Odds Betting Terminals - or 'gaming machines' as they're more commonly referred to. Roulette being the most popular game played. But with each betting shop only being allowed to have a maximum of four of these machines in any one shop, that's the reason why you'll see two or three - four even - of the same betting shop company on the same street, sometimes within the space of just a few hundred yards of each other. Therefore instead of only having *four* gaming machines available on a high street they'll have up to twelve or sixteen. And even though most ordinary people don't have a daily flutter on the horses, a great deal *do* visit the bookies on a daily basis just to play the machines. And this was the reason why it has been highlighted in the news recently, because so many people are becoming hooked on them, particularly on the roulette. These machines can be lethal and they are far more addictive than gambling on the horses and I've seen firsthand just how addictive they are to some people.

I was in the town centre early one Saturday morning and I walked into a betting shop at around twenty past nine to put my bets on for the afternoon. The shop had only opened at 9 o'clock so it had been open for no more than twenty five minutes and there was this guy banging on the roulette machine and effing and blinding at it. He then walked out and went to the cash machine at the bank next door (unfortunately for him it wasn't one of the machines that I sometimes leave money hanging out of!) and he came back in with a handful of ten and twenty pound notes and fed them into the machine. Then no more than two minutes later I heard him shout, "You fucking bastard!" and when I turned around I watched as he started punching the machine and smashed his fist right through the glass. He then grabbed it with both hands and pulled it away from the wall and turned it over and stormed out. And it wasn't even half nine in the morning! That just shows how lethal and addictive they can be and that's why the government stepped in not so long ago and reduced the maximum stake down from £100 to just £2.

I must admit that I felt really sorry for that bloke because he may well have put an entire week's wages in that machine and it probably left him with no money at all. And my first thought was to go after him and ask him how much he'd lost and withdraw the money from the cash machine next door and give it him back. But I didn't because I thought that if I did that he'd more than likely just walk back in the bookies and put it straight back in the machine. Though having said that he wouldn't have been able to because he'd just smashed the machine to smithereens! And he'd have probably been barred anyway, although there were plenty more bookies around for him to go into and put the money into *their* machines, so I thought better of it. I also thought that with him being in the kind of mood that he was in, if I walked up to him and said, "Excuse me.

How much did you just lose on the roulette machine?" His reply might well have been, "What the fuck has it got to do with you, you nosey bastard," and start laying into me like he'd just laid into the machine! So I decided to stay put and not give him any money. Though funnily enough the following Saturday as I was coming out of that same betting shop I did give someone some money. Well, in a roundabout way I did. I didn't actually give it directly to the person but they still benefitted from me giving it someone else on their behalf.

I go to the same betting shop roughly around the same time every Saturday morning. And more or less every time I go I see the same woman either on her way to or on her way back from the launderette opposite carrying her washing, and she always says hello. This particular morning as I came out of the betting shop it was raining and I saw this woman coming out of the launderette and as she walked towards me the handle on the bag she had her washing in snapped and her washing fell out of the bag and onto the wet pavement and dirtied all the clothes she'd just washed.

I know I shouldn't have done really but I started laughing. I couldn't help myself because I thought it was really funny. She heard me laughing and looked at me so I said, "I'm sorry!" and held my hands up in an apologetic manner and added,

"But it *was* quite funny." Luckily she saw the

funny side herself and said, "It's just my luck that!" So I went over and helped her pick her laundry up and asked her how far away she lived and that I'd help her carry it home. She said that she only lived around the corner but said that she'd have to go back in the laundrette and wash it all again. I joked that it must be costing her a fortune going to the laundrette every Saturday and that it'd be cheaper to buy a washing machine and said that it'd also be a lot easier than carrying her washing to the laundrette once a week. And she said that she didn't just go *once* a week, she also went midweek too. And said that she probably could have bought *fifty* washing machines not just one with the money she's spent in the laundrette over the years.

I helped her with her bags back into the laundrette and as she put her washing back into the machine and closed the door she cursed and said, "Damn! I don't believe it! I'm going to have to go home and get another two pounds for the machine." I told her not to bother as I had two quid she could have and took two pound coins out of my pocket and gave them to her. She thanked me and said that she'd give it back to me the following Saturday or when she next saw me. I told her not to worry about it and that I didn't want it back and said it was worth the two quid for making me laugh when her washing fell out of her bag. Again, she saw the funny side.

I then worked out that at £2 a time, twice a

week, she was spending just over £200 a year washing her clothes. And I thought to myself 'I'm sure you could get a washing machine for less than that.'

So she put the two quid in the machine and I asked her how long it'd take and she said that by the time it was washed and she'd put it in the dryer it'd be about an hour. She then cursed again when she remembered she didn't have a pound for the dryer. So I gave her another quid. I spent more in the laundrette that morning than I'd spent in the bookies! She thanked me again and I said bye to her. I also reminded her to check the handles on the carrier bag before she picked it up. And she laughed and sat down and waited for her washing to be done and I left.

The reason I asked her how long her washing would take was because there was a Curry's/PC World that was about a ten minute drive away, so I went back to my car and drove up there. And I went in and asked one of the sales people how much a decent washing machine that also had a tumble dryer built in would cost and he said that they had a Hotpoint one on offer that had just been reduced from £399 to £279. I said that would do and asked how much delivery and fitting would cost and he said that it was an extra £25. So I told him that'd be fine and that I'd pay for it but that it wasn't going to be in my name. I also told him that I didn't know the name of the person whom it was for and just said that it was for a woman and that

I'd get her to come in and give him her name and delivery details etc. He said that'd be okay and that he'd give me a receipt for me to give to her and then all she'd have to do is come in with it and he'd take care of it. So I went with him to the desk to pay and as I handed him my credit card, guess what he asked? "Would you like to take out an extended three year warranty on it!" I looked at him and before I could answer he said, "You usually do." Then I realised. He was the same sales assistant that was serving the old bloke and his wife who I bought the sixty inch plasma TV for about nine months earlier! I replied, "Go on then," and said, "You must love serving me with all the commission you get flogging me extended warranties." He must also have wondered why I buy televisions and washing machines for people I don't even know!

So I got the receipt off him (and he got yet more commission) and I drove back to the laundrette, and when I walked in the woman was still sat there. She looked surprised to see me again so soon. So I jokingly said that I'd been waiting for her to leave the laundrette in the hope the handle would snap on her bag again so I could have another laugh. I then asked her if she knew the Curry's warehouse on the shopping centre a few miles away and she said she did. So I handed her the receipt and said that she no longer had to carry her washing to the laundrette twice a week as I'd bought her a washer dryer and that all she needed to do was to go there and arrange a time for them to deliver it. And similar to the old guy who I bought the television for in Curry's, she too didn't quite know what to say and was rather stunned – and rather pleased.

I haven't seen that woman since, partly because for the following month after that I was out of the country. And also from that day on she had no need to go to the laundrette opposite the bookies every Saturday because she could now do her washing at home. But I did receive a very nice 'thank you' card from her that I picked up around six weeks later when I next went into the betting shop that she'd left behind the counter for me. It didn't have my name on the envelope, obviously, because she didn't know it. It just had a description of me written on the envelope, which like my real name and the area where I live I'm not going to tell you! It also had three one pound coins in it for the one's I'd given her when she had to wash her clothes again. (I still chuckle at that handle snapping even now.) Though as yet I haven't received a thank you card from the sales assistant in Curry's for all the commission I've earned him from the extended warranties I've bought!

Epilogue.

Give or take a few cash giveaways and the odd surprise present here and there, me buying that washing machine for that woman was one of the most recent ones I'd done at the time of writing this book. And by the time this book is written, printed, published and eventually read by people I would've given away yet more money and surprised quite a few others. And as well as giving money *to* and buying things *for* those people I've already told you about, like friendly motorists in car parks that'll give you the money for a ticket, friendly traffic wardens that *don't issue* tickets, nurses with bad backs, smiling waitresses at dog tracks, people that sweep the streets, people that sleep *on* the streets, women that sit outside men's toilets in foreign countries, women with kids at airports that *need to get* to foreign countries, women with kids at train stations that *weren't travelling* to foreign countries but were still making a heck of a journey, paying for someone's M.O.T (all fifty of them) and buying someone a *T.V*, hiding money inside clothes and books and paying for someone's lunch whilst dressed as Worzel Gummidge and getting some very *funny* looks, there are also those that I've *not* told you about because there are far, far too many to mention. But amongst which include leaving a £200 tip for a cleaner in my hotel room, paying for another guests room in the same hotel for no reason whatsoever (I just picked a room number on the same floor and said I'd pay for it as I was checking out) bought someone a car, bought a bloke and his son a season ticket each at Chelsea and paid for a young couple to go on a world cruise for their honeymoon. There are many more too. In fact, I could probably write another book and quite easily fill it with the one's I haven't told you about.

So when will I stop giving my money away? Not that the answer to *when* will I stop giving it away being what you all want to know - you'd probably much rather know the answer to *where next* will I be giving it away! Well the answer to both is, who knows? Even *I* don't know the answer to those two questions and I'm the one giving it away! Though to give you a clue as to where you're most likely to see me, if you live south of junction eight on the M6 you've got a better chance of bumping into me than those that live *north* of junction eight on the M6. And that's all I'm telling you! And if from that needle in a haystack, or rather, from that slip road on the spaghetti junction (which I don't live far from) you can suss out who I am then I *certainly will* give you a few quid.

But I really have no idea when I'll stop. It's indefinite. I could get fed up tomorrow and stop doing it, though I doubt it. The other thing is, that even though I've given away well over a million pounds in the last two years (you'll have to check with Miss X for the exact figure) I've probably made the same amount over the same period. So in effect I've probably not actually given any of my money away at all because what I *have* given away I've recouped from the various business interests I have. So I suppose there may well be some truth in the saying 'money goes to money' after all. And so considering that I've still got the same amount of money now as when I started, I may as well continue giving it away for the foreseeable future.

You may have noticed that I haven't named names or revealed the exact locations (apart from the odd one or two) of where the events I've told you about have taken place. Again, for the safety reasons which I explained about at the beginning, that's so as not to reveal too much of my whereabouts. It may also lead to my true identity being revealed and people finding out who I really am. Although writing in such a cloak and dagger way made me feel as though I was more like Andy McNab than Tom Jones! Though I dare say that the locations, events and circumstances that Andy McNab found himself in (no doubt on occasions with a *real* dagger) and subsequently wrote about, were far more perilous than the ones I've told you about. And one other difference between Andy McNab's books and mine is that he writes his by himself, where I received a fair bit of assistance.

'Why' is a question that I must have been asked a million times whilst giving money to people. Well, maybe not quite a *million* times, that'd be exaggerating it slightly, but I have been asked it a hell of a lot of times nonetheless. And some of you may well be asking *why* yourselves, as in why if I'd rather not draw attention to myself and would rather remain anonymous would I write a book telling everyone what I've done. Well the answer is that it wasn't my idea to write a book. It was someone else's (though it *was* my idea to write it under the name Tom Jones.)

How this book came about was that I was traced by one of the people I gave money to, who saw and remembered the registration plate on my car (which is very easy to remember) and he got my address from it, which is also quite easy to do. He then contacted me by post to thank me for giving him the money. And do you remember when I was saying about how you get a little bit excited when you see the postman coming down the path and then when you pick up your post you see a hand written letter? Well this was one of those occasions, although I didn't actually see the postman coming, I saw him leaving. So I went to get the post, and amongst the usual bills and brown envelopes was a much thicker envelope that had my name and address hand written on the front. So I opened it, which must have taken me around fifteen minutes because it had that much Sellotape wrapped around it. It was like playing a solo game of pass the parcel trying to get it undone! And after I'd stripped away the fourteen rolls of Sellotape that had been used to seal it with and opened the envelope, I found a book inside. It was called 'The Best Husband and Wife Joke Book Ever.' I later found out that a copy of the book was bought as a wedding gift for Prince Harry as a bit of a joke by one of his old army pals.

There was also a note with it that read, 'Thanks for the hundred quid. It wasn't quite enough to repair the dents and scratches on my BM' but I very much appreciated it all the same, and hopefully you appreciate the humour in this book.' It was from the guy in the car park, the one wearing the shorts who gave me a pound for the ticket machine and who was driving a BMW that had scratched paintwork above the wheel arch. So I read the book, which did appeal to my sense of humour, and at the back of it, it gave his website address. It was called Bollocks To Christmas.com. Hopefully Harry didn't leave the book lying around Buckingham Palace. Because if he had of done and his gran had picked it up and flicked through it and saw the web address and logged onto it, *one* certainly *wouldn't* have been amused! Mind you, her speech on Christmas day would be *very* amusing if she used some of the material from it - and probably far many more people would tune in to watch! Although I dare say the Queens speech would have to be moved from its usual slot of 3pm to well after the watershed.

So I took a look at his web site and at the bottom of it was his email address so I contacted him and thanked him for the book. He then replied back and we sent one or two more emails to each other and in one of them he asked if I'd ever thought about writing a book myself. I told him I hadn't and that I wouldn't have a clue where to start and he said that if I fancied having a go to let him know and he'd help me with it. And so after thinking about it and discussing it with my wife who thought it was a great idea (though no doubt she'd have probably said it was a *bad* idea if she'd have known I was going to tell you all about her piles!) I decided to do just that and give it a go. And true to his word he helped me with it and this is the end result. So if you think this book was a load of crap then blame him because it was his idea and he's done most of the work! But hopefully you *didn't* think it was a load of crap and instead you enjoyed reading it just as much as I enjoy brightening up people's day by giving my money to them. And if by chance you're one of those I've given money too or you've received a Christmas card in the post with £200 in it and you're thinking 'That's me he's talking about!' then you're very welcome to it. As is *everyone* who has come by my money in one way or the other, be it I've handed it to you in person, or you've found it in a cash dispenser, or it's fell out of a newspaper you were reading whilst travelling on the Bakerloo line, or if some tramp has walked into your local bistro and plonked it on your table as you were about to order your lunch!

And what better way to finish than with another of my dad's favourite sayings that he must have said to me a thousand times. No, not 'here you go Son, I've put new soles and heels on your school shoes for you again.' His *other* favourite saying, the one *we've all* heard a thousand times before but is still very true: It's nice to be important but it's more important to be nice.

It's also important to appreciate what you've got and when you're fortunate enough to have the kind of wealth that I've got it's nice to be able to share a little bit of it with others.